WITH FACES TO THE EVENING SUN

Faith Stories
from the
Nursing Home

Richard L. Morgan

UPPER
ROOM BOOKS
NASHVILLE

Page 191 constitutes an extension of the copyright page.

Cover Illustration: © Pam Rossi
Interior Design: Putnam Graphics & Media Design
First Printing: April 1998

The Upper Room Web Site: http://www.upperrom.org

The Library of Congress Cataloging-in-Publication Data

Morgan, Richard Lyon, 1929-
    With faces to the evening sun: faith stories from the nursing home / Richard L. Morgan.
        p.   cm.
    ISBN 0-8358-0826-2
    1. Nursing home patients—Prayer-books and devotions—English.
2. Aged—Religious life. 3. Meditations. I. Title.
BV4580.M574 1998
248.8'5—DC21   97-33189
                                                        CIP

Printed in the United States of America

DEDICATION

To Grace and Lindy,
roommates and soul mates
at Grace Heights Nursing Home.
Your shining faces, loving friendship,
and indomitable courage
remain a real faith story.

Contents

I. LEAVING HOME 14

II. SETTLING IN 39

III. ENEMIES OF THE SPIRIT 60

IV. GRACE MOMENTS 79

V. DEFIANT FAITH.................................98

VI. WHEN THE OWL CALLS YOUR NAME ..120

VII. HOME AT LAST................................142

Appendix
  • A Room Blessing for a New Resident....184
  • A Service for Upholding a Resident
    Moving from Independent Living
    to Nursing Care.............................186
  • A Memorial Service for Residents........188

Foreword

For a quarter of a century my ministry has included steady contact with residents at the Beatitudes Campus of Care. This campus, a multilevel retirement facility, is one of the outreach ministries at Church of the Beatitudes. When our congregation was only six years old, leaders determined they would build a complex where older people could live in a stimulating, caring environment. Now the Campus of Care is home to 700 men and women who live in apartments, assisted living units, or the skilled nursing section.

Campus residents enjoy telling a story about two men who were driving past our facility. Noticing a big sign identifying the Campus of Care, the passenger said to the driver, "What does that mean—'Campus of Care'?"

"I'm not sure," the driver replied, but I think it's some sort of nursing home."

"Ugh," responded the first man. "That's the last place I'd want to live."

"And it may be," said the driver.

Indeed, for many people, their last home on earth, and perhaps the last place they'd want to live, is a nursing home. However, no matter how fancy the accommodations or expensive the price tag, there are almost always struggles in adjusting to the nursing home lifestyle. Richard Morgan appropriately recognizes the trauma to the human spirit that often results from moving into such a setting. However, as he sensitively portrays daily thoughts, feelings, and actions of nursing home residents, he does so to the unrelenting rhythm of God's loving presence.

The picture Morgan paints of life in a long-term care environment includes not only the dismal shades but also brighter rays reflecting the glow of faith. Each of the fifty-four meditations are prepared for residents, caregivers, and family members. Each one contains on-target passages from the Bible, arresting commentary, and closing prayer thoughts. Affective quotations enliven the meditations. People appearing on the pages look and sound like the frail people I know at the Beatitudes Campus. My elderly friends too are a combination of gloomy moods plus bursts of hope and even humor.

Dick Morgan's just-right words, beginning with the title, are memorable. In pondering the name of this book, I realized he had chosen three key words that represent his spirit and purpose: *faces, evening* and *sun*.

To speak of "faces" is much more personal than to use a generic term such as occupant or resident. Each unique face records a life-time history; it is an etching revealing decisions, failures, hopes. As I have driven my battery-operated scooter down long halls of our Care Center, I have sometimes felt discouraged by the rows of bodies in wheelchairs lining the corridor. But then I approach a nodding, seemingly lifeless figure. When I call out the name of Wayne or Esther, the slumped body usually responds. The previous expressionless countenance becomes animated.

Each face is as different as never-to-be-repeated snowflakes; the story enshrined in every body is diverse, personal. In the pages of this book we meet individuals like Mary, John, Pauline, and others who talk to us honestly. As sensitively expressed in the meditation "Hope for Mrs. Paper Face," Richard Morgan looks behind masquerades into the hearts of human beings who eventually will see God "face to face."

One of Morgan's earlier books, *Autumn Wisdom*, gently yet powerfully reminds readers that all life moves toward conclusion, to a final season. Likewise, he uses the analogy of *evening* to symbolize life in a nursing home. Evening also brings a sense of closure, a time of coolness.

Here in Arizona, sunsets astound us evening after evening. One of my aged Care Center friends takes delight in watching sunsets every day. "Why, I've never seen the sky look so beautiful," she repeatedly exclaims. Indeed, every sunset is a fresh painting, a new benediction for that day.

This book offers light, power, energy—attributes to the sun. Although we do not worship the sun, we bring praise to God, source of all creation. There will be a sunrise tomorrow, a morning will dawn for us—on this earth or elsewhere in God's continuing care.

Dosia Carlson
Pastor, Caring Ministries
Church of the Beatitudes
Phoenix, Arizona

Preface

We need a new vision of the nursing home where living is something more than not dying. Proverbs 29:18 states, "Where there is no vision, the people perish" (KJV).

With Faces to the Evening Sun provides this new perception as it tells incredible stories of people who have lived with faith and courage in nursing homes. Like the ancient Israelites in Babylon, they have sung the Lord's song in a strange land. Most of these stories are never heard, lost behind the walls of these tribal villages.

Jaber F. Gubrium reports how one nursing home administrator became intentional about recording life stories of residents. He said,

> Ya walk in here day after day, and it's easy to think that all there is to their lives is sitting in wheelchairs, eating, sleeping, and being sick. That's pretty negative. They're just faces in the hall, without stories. I would guess that if you took time to listen, they'd have a lot of interesting things to say about their lives.

Yes, there are incredible faith stories which come from those shuffling down a bare hall, sleeping in chairs, confined to their beds. From the shadowed corners we walk with them from the moment they arrive, through the anxious days and nights of getting settled, until finally they feel "at home." These are faith stories, full of saving humor, defiant courage, and God's grace.

Recall the season of Advent, the celebration of the coming of Jesus Christ to our world. The words of the prophet are heard again, "The people who walked in darkness have seen a great light; those who lived in a land of deep darkness—on them light has shined" (Isa. 9:2). That light that shines in our hearts in the face of Jesus Christ, now shines in the faces of those who sit in darkness and the shadow of death. It is a light no darkness can extinguish. It is a light often obscured by our own blindness. It is a light that family members, church members, the whole world needs to see, the light on those blessed faces to the evening sun.

Prayer of Lancelot Andrewes

The day is over, and I give you thanks,
  O Lord.
Evening is at hand; furnish it with
  brightness.
Do not forsake me now that my strength
  is failing;
But bear me, carry me, deliver me, to my
  old age,
To the time of my white hair. Stay with
  me, Lord, for evening is coming,
And the day of this fretful life is far spent.
May your strength be made perfect in my
  weakness.

Author's Notes

Most names of places are fictional. Most characters in these stories are real persons, but all of their names have been changed to preserve confidentiality. You may recognize some of the people.
You may even recognize yourself some day.

I. Leaving Home

Most people put a very personal imprint on
the place where they live . . .
Self-constituting memories get put into the
walls and fabric of the house . . .
Home is the place to live out a rhythm
of life—
To leave home is to leave an embodied
expression of the self.

Henry C. Simmons and Mark A. Peters

1

Thus says the LORD of hosts, the God of Israel, to all who were carried away captive, . . . Build houses and dwell in them; plant gardens and eat their fruit . . . And seek the peace of the city . . . and pray to the LORD for it; for in its peace you will have peace.

Jeremiah 29:4-5, 7 (NKJV)

It's Up to You

Jeremiah's counsel to the Israelites exiled from their homes to Babylon was to settle down there, find a new home in this strange place, and pray for its peace. These words speak remarkably to anyone who enters a nursing home. For you too know the agony of leaving home and feeling abandoned in a strange place.

For some people, settling in seems an impossibility. They never adjust, and they spend the rest of their days in a constant state of complaint. Others seek nursing homes as a temporary place and hope to go back home within a short time, and some do. Others seethe with anger against their relatives who placed them there, scheme to revoke the power of attorney they surrendered, and escape.

Whatever the case, Jeremiah's letter to the exiles in Babylon seems as if it were written to today's residents of nursing homes. The exiles hoped to return to their homes in Jerusalem, and yet Jeremiah tells them they will be there for a while, to settle in and pray for the peace of the city. This seems good counsel for nursing home residents too.

Ever since the Lord told Adam and Eve to get their baggage together because they were moving out of Eden, human beings have been in a state of transition. So, now you face what seems like the final transition! But how you view this transition can make all the difference.

You may recall the story of a young rabbi who wanted to be acknowledged for his wisdom, but the village people never gave him the honor he expected. When an old rabbi, well-known for his wisdom, came to the village, the clever young rabbi saw this as a grand occasion to show his superiority. This was the young rabbi's plan. Holding a tiny bird in his hand, he would approach the older rabbi and ask a simple question: "Rabbi, is this bird dead or alive?" If the older rabbi said that the bird was alive, the young man would crush the small bird in his hands and show the dead bird to everyone. If the old rabbi said the bird was dead, then the young rabbi would simply open his hands and let the bird fly away. The opportunity soon came for the young rabbi to confront the older rabbi with the foolproof plan. When he asked the old rabbi if the bird was dead or alive, the older man paused for a moment and said, "It's up to you, my friend, it's up to you."

So when you enter a nursing home, you can make the choice to settle in by asking for God's strength and help during this transition. As you seek peace, you will find peace.

Lord of the journey, all through life we face change. But, You, who never change, stay with me in this place and help me settle in. Amen. ⌘

I am forgotten, as good as dead in their hearts, something discarded.

Psalm 31:12 (JB)

Has My Life Come to This?

Katherine had spent the last years since her husband's death in a comfortable apartment. She had caregivers around the clock. But when the cost became too great, with her consent, her daughter had placed her in a nearby nursing home. She had always left her imprint on where she lived. Special furniture and endless "treasures" seemed to define who she was.

On that bleak autumn day, she moved to her new "home." When she entered the room, she looked around and moaned, "Has my life come to this?" No longer was she surrounded by the niceties of her former life. No longer were caregivers ready to heed her every need.

At times choices can be made; when

Medicare or Medicaid is involved, one cannot choose. At times the only available bed is far from home. Rigid routines, dependence on strangers for even the smallest of human needs, and loss of control make the change even harder to bear.

Walter J. Gaffney and Henri J. M. Nouwen wrote in *Aging: The Fulfillment of Life* that older people do experience desolation in later years, especially when they are stripped of their former existence and seem to survive so many of their friends: "Desolation is the crippling experience of the shrinking circle of friends with the devastating awareness that the few years left to live will not allow you to widen the circle again." Sitting in that cold, unfriendly room, an exile from her home, Katherine realized that her life had changed forever.

Katherine's daughter tried to make her room more "homelike"; her favorite chair, an old desk, pictures of her family, and her trusted TV made it seem more comfortable. But Katherine knew all too well that a new chapter of her life had begun that day. She felt like the ancient psalmist, " I am forgotten, as good as dead in their hearts . . . " But to maintain strength, Katherine would have to continue on with the psalmist to verse 14 and realize that she is not alone: "I trust in you, O LORD; I say, You are my God. My times are in your hand . . ."

Dear God, whenever we face strange places and new surroundings, help us to know you are with us. Some of our treasures on earth may be gone, but our true treasure in heaven is safe and secure. Carry us through these strange nights and days, and may they prepare us for life in our heavenly home. Amen.

One who was there had been an invalid for thirty-eight years. When Jesus saw him lying there and learned that he had been in this condition for a long time, he asked him, "Do you want to get well?"

John 5:5-6 (NIV)

Where Time Stands Still

What strikes most people when they enter nursing homes is the way time stands still. There is a sense of timelessness coupled with the various rigid routines that creates a different kind of time. Time drags, and many residents sit in the halls, staring into empty space as clocks on the wall tick away the minutes. Time is like walking on a treadmill; it moves, but nothing ever happens. What really is bewildering is the way residents never speak to one another, thus prolonging time.

That must have been the way the man at the

pool of Bethesda felt. In some ways Bethesda resembled a modern nursing home, for all the sick and invalids gathered there under the shadow of the five porches. This man had lain there for thirty-eight years, a helpless invalid. Perhaps he enjoyed what medicine calls "the secondary gain of sickness," for no doubt he had received attention and help to have survived that long.

Jesus asked the man what appeared to be a crazy question: "Do you want to get well?" Jesus, the great physician, knew that this man had lost the will to be well and needed to be confronted. "Get up! Pick up your mat and walk!" There is no sense in sitting around in this silent time, feeling useless and wanting pity. Get on with life.

It might seem insensitive for people in nursing homes to be confronted with such hard love. Yes, it is difficult, and time does seem to stand still. But Charles Wells provides a fresh perspective on time in *Letters to Myself*:

> Now there is time to look rather than
> to just glance, time to listen rather
> than just hear, time to savor rather
> than just taste, time to relish and

delight in whatever the present may bring . . . There will be time to remember, to recall the experiences you've lived, to live them once again, now with a leisure you never allowed yourself before . . . Take time, old man, take time.

So easy to sit in those endless halls and stare at the large clock on the wall and be tyrannized by time. Jesus wants us to be well in spirit as long as we live. So he confronts us and wants us to be responsible human beings—to redeem the time as Paul wrote in Ephesians 5:16. Despite being in a strange place, make each day count. Then time will fly, not drag.

Lord of time and eternity, forgive us for buying into self-defeating patterns that make time feel like concrete in our shoes. Help us to make each day count; help us to reach out to others in friendship; and may we never forget that even in this place, Lord, you can make every day your time. Amen.

*By faith Abraham obeyed when he was
called to set out for a place that he was to
receive as an inheritance; and he set out,
not knowing where he was going. By faith
he stayed for a time in the land . . . living
in tents.*

Hebrews 11:8-9

When God Blesses Your Space

Moving into a nursing home is a major transition. Giving up your home of many years, a
place of happy memories, is never easy. During
those first few days and weeks, time looms
large and seems always the same. You find
yourself just "passing the time."

Yet, when a person can feel "at home" in his
or her room, it does make a difference. "Place"
always has had special significance in the
history of God's people from that time when
they looked for a homeland to the despair of

exile following their inheritance of a good land. In *Systematic Theology* Paul Tillich expresses that God's grace is always available:

> In the certainty of an omnipresent God we are always at home and not at home, rooted and uprooted, resting and wandering, being placed and displaced, known by one place and not known by any place. And in the certainty of the omnipresent God we are always in the sanctuary.

Abraham and Sarah moved from their comfortable home in Ur of the Chaldees and journeyed to a new place where they lived in tents. Yet, even in this strange place, Abraham built an altar to the Lord.

At Holly Hall Christian Retirement Community in Houston, Texas, a Room Blessing is given to each new resident. (The Room Blessing is found on pages 184–185.) Wesley Stevens says, "It has a close kinship with baptism. It is a sacramental acknowledgment of 'place' and, . . . [an initiation] into the community. [The room blessing] signifies entry into a uniquely Christian way of living together. In a sense, the blessing includes all of the things packed up and brought with her."

Blessing of the room and the things that the resident has brought with her (including the storehouse of memories these possessions recall) is more than a welcoming ceremony. As Abraham built an altar in his new place, so the blessing connotes God's presence in this new place. It helps residents reach the point where they speak of "my room" and hastens the time when they refer to this place as home.

Almighty God, bless this house of many rooms with your presence. May it be a haven of blessing and a place of peace. Amen. ∽

5

[Jesus] said to them, "Take nothing for your journey."

Luke 9:3

Bare Essentials

Everyone who travels knows how important it is to travel lightly. We always ask, "What do we really need for this trip?" Getting rid of excess baggage is a major need for older people. We go from larger homes to smaller ones, from smaller ones to apartments, from apartments to assisted living in one room, from one room to one bed in the health care center. And the major question always is, "What do we take with us?"

Jesus gave explicit instructions to the disciples as they set out on their journey. He warned them that this journey would be difficult and filled with uncertain receptions. His packing tip on that stark journey was to travel light—indeed to take no baggage at all. How often we can recall struggling with our baggage in airports and wondering whether we really needed all these things.

Going to a nursing home means that you must travel lightly for this journey. Preparations to move mean sorting cherished belongings. Even if a private room is available (a rare exception in most nursing homes) it will be too small for any but the most limited possessions. When that choice is made by others, it is really devasting: a couple of cartons, a half dozen dresses or suits, a couple of shelves in a closet. A lifetime in two boxes!

Ray and Margaret were in different rooms in a nursing home, but all they could take with them was a comfortable chair from their old home. Ray muttered, "No sense bringing anything else here, and I know we don't need a suitcase since we won't be going anywhere."

Jesus said, "Take nothing for the journey." Travel light. A favorite chair, treasured pictures hung on the wall, the favorite Bible—these simple things can make the journey easier. Getting rid of excess baggage is good for the soul!

Lord of the journey, when we leave behind so much of our possessions, help us to realize you are our most cherished possession. As the psalmist prayed, "Whom have I in heaven but you? And there is nothing on earth that I desire other than you." May we know it is a gift to live simply, a gift that girds us with grace. Amen. ᔕ

6 Read Genesis 21:8-21

For my life is worn out with sorrow, and my years with sighs. My strength gives way under misery, and my bones are all wasted away.

Psalm 31:10 (NJB)

Trapped Outcasts

Mattie sits by the nurses' station every day with her bags packed to go home. Anxiously she waits for that ride that never comes. She tells everyone that to leave her home was to leave herself. All her memories were woven into the walls and fabric of that place. She tells everyone, "I feel like an outcast here," and then sadly whispers, "I want to go home."

Hagar, the handmaid of Sarah, was cast out into the wilderness of Beersheba. After Isaac was born, Sarah wanted no more of Ishmael or Hagar, her husband's bed partner. So mother and child were sent away from the household at Sarah's request.

Like Mattie, many new residents of nursing homes want to go home. Stripped of their homes and their former identity, they feel trapped. And the sad reality is that this time there seems to be no way out. Life always involves suffering, but somehow we bear it with the hope that it will end, and healing comes. But to experience desolation means to know suffering as a chronic condition with little or no anticipated relief. Visitors can put on blinders to shut out the reality and walk through doors into the sunlight outside, but most residents never leave the home. The unspoken truth is that they are here for the rest of their lives.

Walter J. Gaffney and Henri Nouwen in *Aging* point us to Psalm 31:12 as the way older people feel: "I am forgotten, as good as dead in their hearts, something discarded" (JB). In strong language he writes, "Our society does not have room for the elderly. They are ostracized, excommunicated, expelled like contagious lepers, no longer considered as full members of the human community." Was there any way Mattie could have stayed in her home where her heart remained?

God cared for Hagar and her son, outcasts in the wilderness. They found a home in that desert life. So too for Mattie and countless others God can make "the desert . . . rejoice and blossom" (Isa. 35:1), and a home can be found within the wilderness.

Dear Father, we did not ask to live this long. So often our prayer is, "Lord, why did you keep me here so long?" We want to go home . . . Help us learn to be content and, through Christ find the strength for each day. In your name we pray. Amen. 🌥

*I will both lie down and sleep in peace;
for you alone, O LORD, make me lie down
in safety.*

Psalm 4:8

Sleepless in a Strange Place

Pastor Alan seemed proud of the fact that Laura, a parishioner in the nursing home, read his sermons to her roommate, Grace. However, his joy was short-lived when she told him that Grace had insomnia! That story reminded me of the scene in the book of Esther when King Ahasuerus had a sleepless night, and he ordered the most boring reading possible, the "book of records," to put him to sleep (Esther 6:1).

Older people do suffer from insomnia. The "sundowning syndrome" occurs often in nursing homes. Residents nap during the day, wake up at dinner time, and stay awake during the night. One elderly woman, still bleary eyed from a sleepless night commented, "I am glad that the Bible says in heaven 'there will be no night there,' for my nights never seem to end."

Getting used to a new roommate, listening to laundry carts being shoved through the halls, becoming accustomed to nursing assistants' endless chatter and their barging into the room is no small thing. Sleep is disturbed. Someone once asked an older person how he slept. He replied, "Oh, I sleep like a baby. I awake every three hours and cry!"

The psalmist reminds us that sleep is a gift of God. When we remember that the Lord is our keeper who neither slumbers or sleeps, we can lie down and sleep in peace. When a great windstorm arose on the Sea of Galilee, the disciples were terrified, but Jesus was asleep on a cushion in the stern of the boat (Mark 4:38). It is *not* easy to sleep in strange places surrounded by unfamiliar people. Shakespeare wrote,

> Sleep that knits up the ravell'd sleave of care,
>   The death of each day's life,
>   sore labor's bath,

Balm of hurt minds, great nature's second course,
  Chief nourisher in life's feast,—

Macbeth, act 2, scene 2

Sleeping in a strange place is difficult. It is easy to be preoccupied with negative thoughts and to replay them like a video tape in our minds. But even these sleepless hours can be an opportunity for positive images of God's care and a gentle reminder that the One who is our keeper neither slumbers nor sleeps!

God of the long night watches, help us to trust in you when night comes and it is time to sleep. Give us that childlike spirit that puts our lives in your loving hands, knowing you give your beloved sleep. Amen. 🌩

When Jesus saw his mother and the disciple whom he loved standing beside her, he said to his mother, "Woman, here is your son." Then he said to the disciple, "Here is your mother." And from that hour the disciple took her into his own home.

John 19:26, 27

The Hardest Decision of All

There is no other way. Jerri's parents had stayed in an apartment for a while until their health failed. She had tried to keep them with her, but the emotional strain had become unbearable. Sandwiched between the needs of two teenagers and her aging parents, the question most often asked in the home was, "Who comes first?"

So her best alternative was to place them in a nearby nursing home where they could get the care they needed, and she could find some respite. Placing aging parents in a nursing home is the hardest decision of all for adult children. Vivian E. Greenberg says, "It is something we do not want to think about, and our wish is that our parents live relatively functional lives until they are ninety and then just die suddenly without pain." But reality is that as medical science extends life, more and more aging relatives will be placed in nursing homes.

It is impossible to describe the pain that adult children feel when that day comes. Shame that we have somehow betrayed our parents; anger at them for living so long; and worst of all, guilt because we think we could have done something more.

Recall that moment when Jesus placed his mother's life in the hands of John. His earthly life was ending on the cross; and beyond was a resurrected life. "Woman, behold thy son;. . . Behold thy mother! (John 19:26-27, KJV)."

Jesus lovingly entrusted the care of his mother to John, the beloved disciple. Now John must be her care provider and look after her needs. It is not easy to hand over our loved ones to others' care. Yet, that day comes, and we must let go of this strong bond and trust others to do our work. And we must realize that our best *is* good enough.

As the scriptures say, "And will reassure our hearts before him whenever our hearts condemn us; for God is greater than our hearts, and he knows everything" (1 John 3:19-20).

Loving God, how hard it is for everyone when a loved one has to be placed in a nursing home. We agonize as they enter this strange place and leave their home. Yet, that day does come, and all we can do is leave them in your loving hands and ourselves in your grace. Help us, Lord. Amen.

II. Settling In

The early days and weeks in the nursing
home passed quietly for Louisa.
As they drifted by, she decided that two
things were very important:
remembering from day to day
who she was
and who she had been.

Jeri Lee-Hostetler

9

This man lived in the tombs, and no one could bind him anymore, not even with a chain . . . Then Jesus asked him, "What is your name?" "My name is Legion," he replied, "for we are many."

Mark 5:3, 9 (NIV)

Same as It's Always Been

Slowly they wheeled into the room for their first group meeting. Eleven persons sat around a table in relative silence. The leader asked one lady, "What is your name?" "Same as it's always been," she retorted. Undaunted he asked again, "Tell me your name." And she answered, "Will you respect my name *in this place?*" Assured that he would, she said her name was Margaret and then asked him a question. "Are you here to find someone worse off than you are?" A great friendship began.

Recall the moment when Jesus asked the

tormented man the same question, "What is your name?" No one had asked him for years. He had lived as an outcast in some forsaken cemetery. It may have been that someone he loved was buried in that lonely place, so he lived there, unable to free himself from that memory. Jesus walked with that man into the depths of his soul where no one had been and healed his whole life.

It is easy to lose sight of our identities while in a nursing home. Often we are stripped of our past, and nursing attendants treat us as nonpersons. We become that man in Room 304 or the woman who needs her medication in Room 102.

At times nursing attendants patronize us with names like "Honey" and "Sweetie" and "Baby." But we have dignity and appreciate others calling us by our rightful names—Mrs. Brown or Mr. Jones—until we give permission to call us by our first names.

I liked the way Margaret responded to my question when I asked her name. *"Same as it's always been."* Exactly. Each of us has a life history, and others must see beyond our frailty and present condition to see that history.

Recently, a nurse told me that she had

changed her whole approach to the residents when she read their life stories. "These are not just old people with aches and pains, they are persons with incredible life stories."

When nursing attendants and others realize this, true healing can occur.

Loving God, help us to value and affirm the name of every person we meet, especially those who live in nursing homes where it is so easy to forget who they are. We pray in the name of Jesus, whose Name we never forget. Amen. 〰

10

I waited patiently for the LORD; he turned to me and heard my cry . . . he set my feet on a rock and gave me a firm place to stand.

Psalm 40: 1, 2 (NIV)

All We Do Here Is Wait

Martha had been a resident in the nursing home for a month. She told me, "When I first came here I felt like an old sagging sweater, worn out and no good to anyone. I begged the nurses to let me do something. All we do here is sit around and wait." She went on, "We wait for our medicine; we wait for our meals; we wait for mail; we wait for visitors."

Waiting is never popular in any setting. Our culture demands action. "Fix it now!" "Do something!" "Get going!" These are buzz words of this action-oriented society. The ancient psalmist, however, counseled us to "wait patiently for the LORD . . . "

Visiting in countless rooms in a nursing home, I have often found Bible verses or other quotations hung on the wall. In the article "A Spirituality of Waiting" Henri J. M. Nouwen has penned some words which I wish could be seen by every resident:

> A waiting person is a patient person. The word patience means the willingness to stay where we are and live out the situation to the full in the belief that something hidden there will manifest itself to us . . . patient people dare to stay where they are. Patient living means to live actively in the present and wait there . . . nurturing the moment.

Several weeks later when I visited Martha she seemed more content. "My church has brought me some sewing to do so I don't feel utterly useless anymore," she said, and then added, "But I am learning now to be patient and wait on the LORD." She reminded me of the Mary-Martha story and told me she had been more like Martha in her active life. Now, she was trying to be like Mary, taking time to pray, reflect, read the scriptures, and be still.

As I left her room, deeply blessed by her faith and courage, I thought of words from another psalm, "But I have calmed and quieted my soul, like a weaned child with its mother" (Psalm 131:2). The image is not that of a child restless to find its mother's milk. Rather, it is an older child lying placidly in its mother's arms, a picture brimming with tranquility and peace. "All we *do* here is wait" may be a road to spirituality.

Gracious Lord, we wait for you, patiently, as a child waits for her mother's love. We know you will shelter us with your loving arms. Amen.

A man with leprosy came to him and begged him on his knees, "If you are willing, you can make me clean." Filled with compassion, Jesus reached out his hand and touched the man. "I am willing," he said. "Be clean!"

Mark 1:40-41 (NIV)

Touched with Compassion

No disease was more horrible or unspeakable in biblical days than leprosy. Outcasts to society, shunned by the religious, avoided by everyone, lepers were pitiable people. They merely existed, marking time until they died. Their disconnectedness and isolation made life for them a living hell.

A leper came to Jesus and begged for a touch that would heal his disease. Jesus was moved by compassion, and so broke through a wall of law that had stood inviolate in Israel for hundreds of years. He touched the leper and broke through the barrier that separated outcasts from insiders, the unclean from the clean.

Many of the very old residents in nursing homes, particularly those with mental disorientations, are like that leper. They yell, wander, pace, and nobody wants to be near them. The oriented residents resent and fear their wild behaviors, so they are often segregated and live in isolated places. Visits by family and friends are all too short and infrequent.

Christ would reach out in compassion to these people as he did to the leper. They need someone to listen, to validate their feelings. If no one cares, they withdraw within themselves. Naomi Feil, originator of the Feil Method, a way to help the "disoriented old-old," says, "Validation uses empathy to tune into the inner reality of the disoriented old-old. Empathy, or walking in the shoes of the other, builds trust. . . . With empathy, the validation worker picks up their clues and helps put their feelings into words. This validates them and restores dignity."

It is not more than pity they need, it is compassion they crave. Pity stops and stares;

compassion stoops and shares. Nursing assistants, social workers, family, and friends can validate those whom others shun. In so doing, they mirror the compassion of Christ.

Lord, make possible for me by grace
  what is impossible to me by nature.
You know how little I can bear to suffer,
  how quickly I am discouraged
  by a little trouble.
I pray that I may accept and even love
  all the troubles you permit
  to come to me.
To suffer for you and be
  troubled for you
  is good and profitable for my soul.

Thomas á Kempis

12

But no one says, "Where is God my Maker,
who gives songs in the night?"

Job 35:10 (NKJV)

Songs in the Night

Mary was settling into the nursing home, but the hardest part was getting adjusted to nighttime. During the day she kept busy, and she stayed in touch with friends and family by telephone. She enjoyed watching television and listening to the radio for they were her lifelines to the outside world. But the nights were difficult.

Mary found that night was a prime time for prayer. She began to pray for others, as well as for herself. She relived many of her life experiences, especially the happy times. It was almost a miracle that the present could be displaced with treasured memories.

Mary also used the nighttime to plan her days. She knew life in a nursing home would be made up of a parade of irritating occurrences, and in most instances, where she would be powerless. Not since she had been an infant had she been so out of control of her life. So she would plan how to retain some control of her daily life.

Mary's nighttime experience reminds us that God can give songs in the night. And the older we are the more inspiring our song. The following story of two organists illustrates this. Two organists played the same music, and yet people felt drawn to the older one. The younger said to the older organist, "I heard you play today. I could have played every note you played, but somehow my music was not like yours. Your whole soul seems to escape into the melody."

The older man smiled and replied, "You are right. My soul is in my music . . . As you grow older and suffer more, your soul will grow also. As it does, it will fill your music with a unique beauty all your own."

Help us to realize, O God, that what we suffer gives us music in the night and tunes our hearts to love thee. Amen. ᏅᏁ

A loyal friend is a powerful defence: whoever finds one indeed has found a treasure.

Ecclesiasticus 6:14 (NJB)

Soul Friends

When Ellie first came to the nursing home she felt scared and lonely. She was never one to complain, however, so she kept her pain to herself. She always turned to her old Bible for comfort, and she found a passage from the Book of Job that spoke to her soul.

> My days pass: more swiftly than a runner . . . they flee away with never a glimpse of happiness, they skim past like a reed canoe. . . . If I decide

*Ecclesiasticus is found in the Apocrypha in Protestant transla-
tions of the Bible. It is part of the writings between the Testaments.*

to stifle my complaining, change countenance, and wear a smiling face, fear seizes me at the thought of all my woes (Job 9:25-28, NJB).

Ellie thought to herself, "I can really sympathize with Job. I just can't wear a 'smiling face' when I am so scared. Those nurses can put all the yellow smiling faces they want on my door. It doesn't take away my woes."

Then Helen became Ellie's roommate. Helen was a stroke victim, and her communication was unintelligible. She reminded Ellie of a poem she once read. A few stanzas of the poem state:

> Sinking, sinking within her chair
> arms, she sits alone;
>   absorbing another day
>   into her shrunken frame.
>
> Her hands smooth and pluck,
> fold and crease,
>   conditioned by long days
>   of household toil.
>
> . . . .

Her words are a kaleidoscope
of sound, images that break
   into new images,
    a continuity of discontinuities.

But Ellie did more. She constantly spoke to Helen, tried to understand her scattered thoughts, and went with her everywhere. Beyond the puzzled maze of her disrupted mind, Helen reached out to Ellie and they became soul friends. As the writer of Proverbs said, "It is for adversity that a brother [sister] is born" (Proverbs 17:17, NJB). Soul friends.

Help us, O Savior Friend, to find new friends in this place. It is you who bind us fast to another and make us one. Amen.

14

When they had gone ashore, they saw a charcoal fire there, with fish on it, and bread. . . . Jesus said to them, "Come and have breakfast."

John 21:9, 12

Mealtime Memories

It is mealtime in the nursing home. Many of the residents sit, waiting to be fed. Outside it is bleak midwinter and snow is everywhere, like the snow-white hair of these wizened people.

Henry sits at a corner table by himself and waits for his wife. He seems aloof from others and somewhat embarrassed by his wife. She has Alzheimer's and walks the halls with that starched look of mingled confusion and despair. She takes her seat across the table from him; they stare at each other, but never speak. One wonders if they recall happier mealtimes.

Mildred waits for her bib. She is now 101 years old and yet tells everyone she is 62. No one speaks to her silence. She had been dietician at a school for the hearing impaired. We wonder what memories are buried in her mind from serving endless meals for deaf children. Now others serve food to her.

George wheels into the dining room with that perpetual scowl on his face. He is only 56 and wants to go home. The nurses say he is a perpetual nuisance, but underneath that rough demeanor is a person who needs attention. When someone mentions his birthday is next week, the scowl turns into a smile.

Bertha and Harriet are friends. Unlike other residents who sit in stony silence waiting to be fed, these ladies chatter back and forth. Bertha has arranged the flowers on the table with loving care. Harriet recalls the days when she was an Avon lady and she ate most of her meals on the run.

Gingerly, the aides slip bibs around most of the residents, and their variegated food is brought to them. Some are fed; others feed themselves, their silence broken only by the clatter of dishes and the chatter of two friends.

Jesus ate many meals with his friends. After the resurrection, he cooked breakfast for them on the Lake of Galilee. Eating was sacramental, a time when God's presence was real. Was the scene in the nursing home really that different?

O Thou who feds the hungry multitudes, who carries old people in your heart, may your presence sanctify meals in a nursing home. Amen. ⏥

15

When the entire nation had finished crossing over the Jordan, the LORD said to Joshua: "Select twelve men from the people . . . and command them, 'Take twelve stones from here out of the middle of the Jordan, . . . carry them over with you, and lay them down in the place where you camp tonight. . . . So these stones shall be to the Israelites a memorial forever."

Joshua 4:1-2, 7

Mementos of Home

After the Israelites had crossed the Jordan, God commanded Joshua to select twelve men, one from each tribe, who would then take twelve stones from the middle of the river and lay them down in the place where they camped in their new situation. The stones were then set up in Gilgal (circle of stones). In future days, when children asked what these stones meant, the parents would answer, "Israel crossed over the Jordan here on dry ground . . . the hand of the LORD is mighty" (Josh. 4:22-24).

Nor was this the only time stones evoked memories of sacred moments. When Israel renewed its covenant with God at Shechem, Joshua wrote the covenant and "took a large stone, and set it up there in the sanctuary of the LORD" (Josh. 24:26).

When we moved to a new home, one of the prized possessions that went with us were twelve stones which I had carefully placed in our garden. I had collected each stone from some significant place we had visited, including places from my childhood. These stones evoked memories of who we were, and they brought the past into the present.

As residents, we can take very little into our new space. But some mementos from home need to be there. For you it might be a faded wedding picture, reminding you of young love. For your roommate it is an old chair, reminiscent of comfort spent there. For others it is an afghan or a picture of home, or old books or sewing baskets. All remind us of who we were . . . and are.

Indeed, like the stones at Gilgal, they have sacramental overtones. They make our new place less of a hospital room and more of a home.

Lord Jesus, you took common bread and wine and made a sacrament, a memorial of your death. May some "stones" from our past be with us in this place to remind us of who we are and whose we are. Amen. ᖆ

III. Enemies of the Spirit

If you should go to a nursing home, the last
way station in life's journey, . . .
you must accept it as the last and most
difficult challenge of your life.
And while there, you must play the role
of "happy camper" to the very end—
. . . to preserve your own self-esteem
and dignity.

Charles Wells

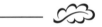

16

Do not cast me off in the time of old age; do not forsake me when my strength is spent. . . . So even to old age and gray hairs, O God, do not forsake me."

Psalm 71:9, 18

Useless . . . Like an Old Ford in the Parlor

Kenneth J. Foreman tells how the *Ford Times* (June 1950) recorded the story of the time Farmer Brown and his wife bought a Ford in 1909. The only place where the Ford could be preserved from dust and rust was their parlor. So, for forty years the Ford stayed in the parlor. They had good intentions of taking it out on the road, but the country roads in that era were bad, and the car would keep its looks longer in the parlor than out on the roads. A hired worker polished the car weekly, and the owners admired its shine. But it never got out on the road, so it was virtually useless.

Many residents in nursing homes can relate to that Ford: They feel patronized by some, played with by many activities, and polished by modern medicine, but never of any real value. One older man kept pacing up and down the halls of a nursing home, muttering repeatedly to himself (and to anyone who would listen), "I feel so useless. Won't somebody give me something to do?"

Even when older people become less mobile, as long as they remain in their own homes, they feel useful. Daily chores, ordinary errands, and other customary rituals maintain a sense of usefulness. But transported to a nursing home often leaves them devastated and feeling they are of little worth to anyone.

For some people, faith is kept in too many parlors. Too many are afraid to expose their faith to dust and dirt. They fear it may be scratched or damaged so they polish it up once a week and admire it. But faith is meant for the open road. It only becomes real when tested by all that life brings.

Residents of nursing homes can make their faith work in a new situation. No longer confined to a church building or the usual places for religion, faith can become a vital aspect of one's life. One resident even commented, "I never knew I had real faith until I came here. Now it is my faith that sustains me, . . . that gets me through every day. She didn't feel useless. . . . The radiance of her faith was known by everyone; despite her frailties she brightened everyone's day with her spirit. Her Ford had been taken out of the parlor into the halls and rooms of that place.

Gracious God, it is so easy to talk the talk and not walk the walk. Help us to get our faith out of the parlor onto the roads of everyday life. Amen.

I am like an owl of the wilderness, like a little owl of the waste places. I lie awake; I am like a lonely bird on the housetop.

Psalm 102:6, 7

I'm So Lonely Here

He kept turning on the call light beside his bed. So, as his nurse, I responded to his every call. But when I visited him, he had no immediate or apparent need. Finally, after many "dry runs," I said, "Listen, that call light is only for emergencies. I just can't keep running in here when you have no special needs." "But I do," he replied, "I'm terribly lonely here." So I made a deal with him. If he would stop turning on the call light, I would come and spend some time with him, and we would just visit together. He agreed. He never turned on the call light again.

I heard that story from a male nurse in one of my groups. He told me how this man was lonely and needed attention. That story reminded me of the psalmist's lament: "I am like a lonely bird on the housetop."

What makes the loneliness of the elderly different is that the emptiness grows out of a loss as well as a need. When more loved ones are dead than living, when cherished friends have left this world, one feels acute loneliness.

Our friend who kept turning on the call light found some answer to his loneliness by the companionship of the nurse. Nothing is more heartbreaking than to hear an older person say, "I have nobody." But this is where faith and prayer enter. Jesus said to the disciples on the night when He physically left them, "I will not leave you orphaned" (John 14:18).

Another answer is a vital prayer life. In *Aging in the Lord* by Sr. Mary Hester Valentine, she tells of an eighty-year-old woman, who said, "I used to talk to myself. . . . One day it struck me: God is within me. Why don't I talk with him? Now I have most personal and private conversations with him. I tell him everything. I even complain."

So the answer to loneliness is to find a creative balance between being with others and being alone. But with God, we are never alone.

Loving God, I do feel so all alone at times. I long for the gentle touch of friends. They seldom visit me. In my long night watches be present for me. Amen. ᵹ

18

And be kind to one another, tender-hearted, forgiving one another, as God in Christ has forgiven you.

Ephesians 4:32

When Roommates Fight

Robert and Charlie were roommates and got along well. That is, until the day of the big fight. Both had won medals for participating in the Senior Games and proudly wore those medals in the nursing home. Charlie, a World War II veteran, sat outside his room in a wheelchair as if he were still standing guard duty. Robert was more sociable and usually wheeled around to visit other residents. His presence was known throughout the facility by his raucous and contagious laughter.

One day Robert was wearing his medals, and Charlie (forgetting where he had placed his) accused Robert of stealing his medals.

Words ensued, and the angry old men began shoving one another from their wheelchairs. Only the intervention of the chaplain prevented them from a worse altercation.

For days neither spoke to the other but glared with obvious hostility from across his part of the room. Robert told the chaplain he had found a verse of the Bible which gave him guidance. Pointing to Proverbs 24:1 he read, "Do not envy the wicked, nor desire to be with them." "I just keep out of his way," he said, "because if I get too near him, I might take a poke at him."

Days followed, marked by that awful silence of alienation. Finally, the activities director ended the impasse. She discovered where Charlie had placed his medals, and she convinced him that Robert had not stolen from him. With some reluctance, Charlie apologized to Robert. Gnarled hands reached out from steel chairs to bridge the chasm between them. In time, they began to speak to each other. We knew that the rift had been healed when they finally could laugh about it.

One of the difficult aspects of being in a nursing home is sharing a room with someone else. It is never easy to share your space with a stranger. Conflicts are inevitable, but forgiveness brings reconciliation.

Several months later, Charlie died. Robert mourned the loss of his friend and said, "It was so important that we made peace with each other over those silly medals. I would not want Charlie to have died without making up with him. Instead of feeling guilty over our conflict, I remember how we became friends again." Broken relationships can be healed!

Dear God, can I dare to make this my prayer? Lord, treat me tomorrow, as I have treated my neighbor today.
Amen.

19

Read 1 Kings 19:1-18

Why be so downcast, why all these sighs?
Hope in God! I will praise him still, my
Saviour, my God.

Psalm 42:5-6 *(NJB)*

The Worst of the Dwindles

Dr. Anne Egbert, a geriatrician, claims that common ailments associated with aging may be called "dwindles" or "the failure to thrive." As people become elderly, some appear to dwindle away, becoming caught in a downward emotional and physical spiral that often leads to death.

Depression is the worst of the dwindles. It involves a shutting down of the human spirit. In depression, the spirit wilts and no longer reaches out to others or God. Many residents of nursing homes suffer from depression and sink into despair.

At the end of his life, the prophet Elijah suffered from the dwindles. Traveling to Beersheba, he entered the desert beyond. There, in the depths of depression, he sat down in the inadequate shade of a broom shrub and longed for death. "It is enough; now, O LORD, take away my life." But God sent an angel to cheer him on. Food and drink were provided, and Elijah was strengthened for the long trip over the desert to Horeb, the mount of God. At this sacred place, where Moses had established the covenant between Yahweh and Israel, Elijah found God in the soft whisper, and his life was restored.

Philip also had the dwindles. His wife had died unexpectedly while undergoing surgery; his daughter, who had promised to care for him, was going through a separation, so she had placed him in a health care center. He cried a lot. He ate like a bird and found sleep evasive. When his friends visited him, he spent most of the time bemoaning his fate and wringing his hands. Philip had all the symptoms of the "dwindles" . . . a lack of appetite, declining energy, and reclusiveness.

But Philip got help. He talked to a counselor; he took medication for his depression. He called friends, and he began to rebuild his shattered life. And he said, "God has not given up on me, yet. There is still hope." No doubt, his "dwindles" were dwindling.

Restore unto us, O Lord,
the joy of our salvation. Amen. ᑓ

20

Read 1 Corinthians 10:1-13

No testing has overtaken you that is not common to everyone. God is faithful, and he will not let you be tested beyond your strength, but with the testing he will also provide the way out so that you may be able to endure it.

1 Corinthians 10:13

Eight Tons and One Bluebird

In *Candles on Glacier* Kenneth J. Foreman recalls in the *New Yorker* a series of pictures showing a sign by a bridge plainly marked "Load Limit Eight Tons." Approaching the bridge was a truck, also marked "8 Tons" on its side. When just about in the middle of the bridge, a bluebird alighted on the truck. Suddenly, the bridge collapsed, bridge and truck crashing into the river below. The bridge was built for eight tons; the truck's weight was precisely eight tons. The bridge load limit was literal. It could not hold eight tons and one bluebird.

Of course, the story may be fictional. Most bridges could stand up under their limit and probably a few bluebirds extra. But any bridge in the world has its breaking point somewhere. And there comes a point where we reach our breaking point too.

Many residents in nursing homes feel they have reached their "breaking point." Life has brought them "eight tons," and living in a nursing home seems like that "one bluebird" that tips the balance.

Paul's counsel for the struggling Corinthians seems addressed to persons in nursing homes. God does not allow us to be tested beyond our endurance, and when we face difficult times, God provides a way through the trouble. We may not get *out* of our troubles, but God enables us to get *through* them! I remember a grace moment when former Senator Sam J. Ervin recited Annie Johnson Flint's poem before a gathering of church people.

God hath not promised
Skies always blue,
Flower-strewn pathways
All our lives through;
God hath not promised
Sun without rain,
Joy without sorrow,
Peace without pain.

But God hath promised
Strength for the day,
Rest for the labor,
Light for the way,
Grace for the trials,
Help from above,
Unfailing sympathy,
Undying love.

Lord, life is hard. I seem so hemmed in by my troubles, but you promised a way through. Give me grace for this day . . . and night. Amen. ⌒⌒

*You number my wanderings; put my tears
in Your bottle; are they not in Your book?*

Psalm 56:8 (NKJV)

Bottled Tears/Moving On

James was visibly upset. He had just learned that due to restructuring of the nursing home, he would be moved from the room where he had lived for six years. He had finally grown accustomed to his place where he could slump in his easy chair and read the paper and from his window watch birds come to his feeder. He knew all his nurses by name, and he loved the relative quiet at the end of the hall. Now all that would change.

When his wife tried to console him, he began to sob. "I just cannot go through another change," he blurted. And then somewhat ashamed at his tears, he suddenly remembered what the psalmist had written when he was sad: "Put my tears in Your bottle." He recalled his preacher telling him that it was an old custom to collect the tears of the family and preserve them in a bottle. When death or serious trouble occurred, each member of the family brought his or her tear bottle and collected tears from all present. These bottles were sacred to the family, because they represented the sorrows of the family. Each person was buried with his or her tear bottle. James thought for a moment. "I do remember that old custom, but what I forgot was that they buried those tears in a bottle. I'm not dead yet, but it's time to move on. God knows where."

My heart ached for him as his wife pushed him in his wheelchair back to his old room. I wondered if being moved against his will wasn't a denial of his rights. His comfort zone had been disrupted. His one sense of security had been snatched from him by a bureaucratic decision. But he had no choice, at least for the moment.

Life brings interruptions and disruptions even when you think you have made your last move. Happy to say, James faced change with that undaunted courage that had characterized his whole life. We moved his comfortable recliner to his new room and transplanted the bird feeder outside his window. He began to learn the names of his new nurses.

Later on, the state inspectors cited the administration for this denial of his rights. When they asked James if he wanted to move back to his old room, he shook his head and said, "No, I have learned in whatever room I am to be content." Somehow his words reminded me of another man named Paul who said similar words from a Roman jail (Philippians 4:12).

God of change, stir us up from our placidness. Help us to know we can do all things through Christ who strengthens us. Amen. 🍃

IV. Grace Moments

"My grace is sufficient for thee." Upon that great word many a weary head has rested; many wounded hearts have been healed by it; discouraged souls have heard its infinite music . . . Grace is the fact of the heart of God.

G. Campbell Morgan

Am I not allowed to do what I choose with what belongs to me? Or are you envious because I am generous? So the last will be first, and the first will be last.

Matthew 20:15-16

Eleventh Hour Grace

The cries of the workers who had labored through the heat of the day seemed justified. They grumbled against the landowner because his payment of wages just didn't seem fair. Why should those who began to work at the eleventh hour get the same pay as those who had borne the burden of the day and the scorching heat? But the landowner reminded them that although it didn't seem fair, it was his way.

God's grace transcends our human understanding. God stands with all the wrong people for the right reasons. And it just doesn't seem fair. Nice guys finish last. Caregivers don't receive care, and people who have served God all their lives end up in nursing homes. Precious people are stricken with devastating illness—it all just doesn't seem fair.

Yet, even when life isn't fair, God is merciful and loving. God's grace comes at unexpected times, in unexpected ways.

She was such a poor woman. All she had in this world was her bed and sheets (on a good day they were clean). All her life possessions were stuffed under her pillow. She told me how God had remembered her in this lonely place. She told me about her faith. I stood there awkwardly . . . listening to a faith that made me uneasy. It was like hearing a foreign language, expressions of belief that went beyond any language. After a few minutes I told her I had to go. Her faith made me ashamed. I felt like Peter when he confronted the reality of God in Christ, and he cried, "Go away from me, Lord, for I am a sinful man!" (Luke 5:8). She smiled and eased my discomfort. "I may never see you again," she said, "but I will certainly see you in the kingdom of heaven."

Grace at the eleventh hour. Grace so big we cannot even see it. Love so inclusive we can't even stand it. A touching moment of grace holding the frail hand of this faith-filled lady— in her eleventh hour.

Generous God, may we never be so proud as not to see your grace in others, or so righteous we forget how poor and needy we really are. Amen.

So he set off and went to his father. But while he was still far off, his father saw him and was filled with compassion; he ran and put his arms around him and kissed him.

Luke 15:20

God's Prodigal Love

Strange, isn't it, how we call this story of Jesus, "the parable of the prodigal son?" In reality, the spotlight of the story falls on the father, not the two sons. We might properly call the story, "the parable of God's prodigal love."

The father loved both sons. His love was unconditionally given to the younger son who was lost in a far country and knew it. His love also embraced the older son who was lost at home but didn't know he was lost. The words of Frederick W. Faber's hymn catch a glimpse of this prodigal love:

> For the love of God is broader
> than the measure of our mind;
> and the heart of the Eternal
> is most wonderfully kind.

Henri J. M. Nouwen, reflecting on Rembrandt's portrait "Prodigal Son," notices the father's hands. His left hand is muscular and strong while his right hand is soft and tender. His left hand wants to stroke and caress. It has gentleness with a firm hold. Nouwen says,

> The Father is not simply a great patriarch. He is mother as well as father. He touches the son with a masculine hand and a feminine hand. He holds, and she caresses. He confirms and she consoles. He is indeed, God, in whom both manhood and womanhood, fatherhood and motherhood, are present.

God's father-mother love *is* prodigal. It shocks us to think that God discards all dignity to lavish that love on us. The inscription on a beautiful stained glass window of a church in south Philadelphia reads: *Come to the mercy seat*. A light shines from that window so street people (the prodigal people) can see it and know God's mercy is for them. But the light shines on the inside in the sanctuary where elder sons and daughters sit in their self-righteous seats, and it says to them, "God loves you too."

Refardless of where one is—at home or in a far country—this incredible story that Jesus told reverberates with one message: God's prodigal love.

Whether we are lost in some far country, or lost at home; whether we know we are lost, or indifferent to our spiritual need, O Loving God, surround us with this prodigal grace. And we will be home as if for the first time. Amen.

24

Read 1 John 4:7-21

The L<small>ORD</small> appeared to him from far away.
I have loved you with an everlasting love;
therefore I have continued my faithfulness
to you.

Jeremiah 31:3

Tenacious Love

He had been a Methodist minister for over fifty years. Some years after his retirement, a stroke had ravaged him, and one side was paralyzed. Every Sunday he wheeled into the chapel for our worship service, and though his speech was slurred, he always had a word for us.

We were singing old hymns, and one of them was George Matheson's "O Love That Wilt Not Let Me Go." Suddenly, the minister stopped our singing and, with halting speech, told the story of how this hymn came to be.

George Matheson was totally blind by the

time he was eighteen. Nevertheless, he became one of Scotland's best-known preachers who had an extraordinary memory that helped him in his preaching. It is said that his fiancee broke their engagement when she learned he was blind.

On his sister's wedding day, Matheson (perhaps recalling the memories of his fiancee who had abandoned him) penned the words of the hymn in five minutes!

> O Love that wilt not let me go,
> I rest my weary soul in thee;
> I give thee back the life I owe,
> that in thine ocean depths its flow
> may richer, fuller be.

What a story! We may be abandoned by family or friends, but there is a Love, the love of God, which never lets us go. That is what Jeremiah realized in the sad, final days of Israel's existence. God's love was their only hope, an everlasting love that would not let the nation ultimately be surrendered to its own sinful folly.

This is the incredible love of God which Jesus revealed. A love that nothing could destroy. Even as religious men nailed that love to a cross, Jesus could pray, "Father, forgive them; for they do not know what they are doing" (Luke 23:34).

What a moment of grace in a worship service where frail elderly people gathered who had been let down by life. That elderly Methodist minister brought a grace moment to those assembled as his shaky voice told the story of a love that will not let us go.

Eternal Love, others let us go.
We are often forgotten, forsaken, and
abandoned. But yours is a love that never
lets us down, and never lets us go.
Nothing can separate us from your love.
Praise God! Amen. ᕙ

25

Bless the LORD, O my soul, and all that is within me, bless his holy name . . . who redeems your life from the Pit.

Psalm 103:1,4

God Moves in a Mysterious Way

Most of them sat in silence as I told the story. One dear lady, a victim of Alzheimer's disease, kept mumbling a language no one understood. It was a strange congregation, interrupted often by nurses giving individuals their pills. I told the story of William Cowper's hymn. His mother died when he was six years old, and he had a troubled childhood. Subject to recurring bouts of depression, he later moved to Olney to be near John Newton, a warm and constant friend. They began to write hymns.

On one occasion, William Cowper asked a driver to take him to the river Ouse. He fully intended to end his life. But a fog developed and when the fog lifted Cowper was in front of his own home. Assured that this was God's providence and mercy, he sat down and wrote the words of the hymn:

> O God, in a mysterious way
> Great wonders You perform;
> You plant Your footsteps in the sea
> And ride upon the storm.
>
> O fearful saints, fresh courage take;
> The clouds you so much dread
> Are big with mercy, and shall break
> In blessings on your head.

I told the story of Joseph, who had been sold into slavery by his own brothers and abandoned in a strange land. Yet God's providence was at work in his life. I told them of how Paul wanted to go to Asia, but never got there; and yet God's plan was for Paul to bring the gospel to Europe and to us. I told them other stories of how God had worked through sorrow and troubles to bring good in people's lives.

But I wondered if anyone really heard. Most of them sat with glazed looks and blank stares.

Then, Mrs. B., who came every Sunday carrying her teddy bear and who usually muttered words only she understood, motioned to me. She looked at me and spoke clearly these words, "God does move in a mysterious way, his wonders to perform. I know." Then she slipped back into her mumbled language. But for a moment, she understood.

God does move in mysterious ways.

Amazing God, you have broken through the worst barriers of old age, and you have helped one, elderly woman know your mercy. Incredible! Amen. ᔆᔆ

26

Read Psalm 77

I have considered the days of old, the years of ancient times . . . And I said, "This is my anguish, But I will remember the years of the right hand of the Most High."

Psalm 77:5,10 (NKJV)

The Best Birthday Party Ever!

We gathered in the Activities Room to celebrate Naomi's 100th birthday. Someone brought a cake, and helpers brought colored balloons and tied them to the residents' wheelchairs. Everyone told his or her age, and we discovered the average age of the group was eighty. The room seemed laden with despair. Many of the residents were sluggish from medication. One resident murmured, "We'd better celebrate our birthdays. The shape we're in we'll probably not have any more."

Another told Bob Hope's old joke: "You can

92

tell you're getting old when the candles cost more than the cake!" Stares met that statement.

Then it was time to sing "Happy Birthday" to Naomi, and although she seemed indifferent to the festivities, a smile creased her face as we sang with gusto. Amazing how these fragile people could still appreciate a birthday party and for a moment forget their aches and pains.

As I left the party, carrying some of the balloons with me, some of them escaped my grasp and soared into the cloudy sky. As I watched them go out of sight, I thought how appropriate. The last song we had sung by request was, "What a friend we have in Jesus, all our sins and griefs to bear." No one could deny the reality of pain present among those people, but for one shining moment there was celebration and joy.

Psalm 77 reminds me of our unusual birthday party. It begins with a lament and ends like a hymn. In his trouble the psalmist cries out to God day and night without being comforted. He meditates upon God's former mercies and is constrained in the midst of present distress to ask, "Will the LORD spurn forever?"

But then the psalmist remembers "the years of the right hand of the Most High." In the first part of the psalm, the focus is on the psalmist's problems, as the psalmist uses the personal pronoun twenty-two times. But there is a shift in focus in the second half of the psalm: God is the supreme thought in the mind of this person. Lament has given way to celebration. As the psalmist counts his years, his birthdays, they are "years of the right hand of the Most High." All our sorrows, disappointments, and infirmities are in God's hand. Then birthdays in a nursing home turn from lament to celebration!

Our constant Friend, whatsoever the years have brought to us, they have been the years of the right hand of the Most High. O Lord, we celebrate our years with you. Amen.

27

I thank my God every time I remember you, constantly praying with joy in every one of my prayers for all of you, because of your sharing in the gospel from the first day until now.

Philippians 1:3-5

The Little Brown Church in the Vale

It happened one dark, dreary Sunday afternoon as we gathered in the nursing home chapel for worship. The dismal weather outside seemed to affect the spirits of the residents as they sat listless and still. Suddenly, Mrs. McGimpsey blurted out, "Let's sing an old song. Why not 'The Church in the Wildwood'? It reminds me of my little church in the country."

"Yes," Mrs. Johnson replied, "I used to play the old pump organ in our church, and that song was my favorite." So I put aside my carefully prepared homily, and we sang this song.

I remembered that William Savage Pitts, who wrote "The Church in the Wildwood," had a dream that one day members of The Congregational Church in Bradford, Iowa, would have a permanent place of worship. The members held services, in homes, a store and other locations, but Pitts envisioned building a brown church in the valley. He pointed to a grove of trees in Bradford's lowland and decided to call the church, "The Church in the Vale."

Haunted by his vision of "a little brown church in the vale," he wrote the hymn, and two years later in 1864 the church was built. Somehow the song triggers memories in older people of childhood churches, reminiscent of that church in Philippi which Paul so dearly loved. Later that night, reflecting on that moment of grace, I wrote these words:

It is raining outside.
Through the fog and cold
I hear the pianist playing,
"The Church in the Wildwood."
The residents are singing, an
  unusual chorus.

God and I sit in the chapel,
Listening to the singing and
   the rain.

. . . .

That song stirs memories in old
   hearts
Of childhood days, of little brown
   churches in the wildwood
When life was simpler and sweeter
And God ever near.
I have residents. God has children.
My residents sing.
God's children praise.
Or, so it seemed to me on that
Dark, damp day in March,
As they sang again and again,
"No place is so dear to my
   childhood
As the little brown Church in the
   vale.
Oh, come, come, come, come, come
   to the church in the wildwood."

*Loving God, help us to sing an old song
in a new way. Amen.*

V. Defiant Faith

Through faith . . . losses have been
transformed into transitions,
new life has emerged out of old,
resurrection has followed death.
Thus these rare people now come
to the end of their lives
with a measure of assurance that the
same God who brought them through
all of life's previous losses will also walk with
them through this final loss, together into the
world beyond.

R. Scott Sullender

28

Some friends play at friendship but a true friend sticks closer than one's nearest kin.
Proverbs 18:24

Celebrating New Friends

Grace spent most of her days and nights in bed in the nursing home. At the age of ninety-two, she had survived two heart attacks and a broken neck which forced her to wear a halo for several months. She seemed listless, content to merely exist for whatever time was left for her. Occasionally she cracked the silence with her inimitable wit, often keeping the nurses in stitches! But for the most part, life had become a whimper.

She gave permission for me to record her life story. Listening to her childhood memories of those halcyon days when life was orderly and uncluttered and hearing the rest of her story was holy ground. But when I asked her about family, she said, "Now I have no family, only the church."

Lindy became her new companion in Room 126. For years Lindy had battled a serious spinal injury which left her bedfast. She was only forty years old but was possessed by a constant curiousity about life, and a gentle, kind spirit. Soon, these roommates became friends. Lindy read to Grace, and they talked endlessly about life. No two people could have had a stronger bond. The transformation in Grace was amazing. From her bed, she joked with the pastors, her nurses, and called Lindy, "my girl." No one who entered that formerly dismal room could help but experience the joy and love that flourished between those two women.

On one sad day, Grace had another heart seizure and died. What intrigued everyone was not the memories of her younger days, but the lingering experience of joy she had given to all in that nursing home.

Jesus told his disciples on the night before his death that they were no longer his servants, but his friends. There is a friendship in Christ that transcends earthly ties and can become genuine even in the midst of sickness and pain.

Grace and Lindy had found that healing relationship, and they transformed the darkness of night into the light of day.

Teach us, compassionate God, that true friendship does not depend on where we are but who we are. We give thanks for all those in our life stories who have blessed our lives with such friendship. Amen. 🌥

29   Read Acts 16:16-34

About midnight Paul and Silas were praying and singing hymns to God, and the prisoners were listening to them.

Acts 16:25

A Night Interlude

It was a long, wintry night at Grace Manor, and Nurse Sue was making her rounds. Except for an occasional moan or cry in the dark, the night was quiet. Millie wandered into the hall, looking around with a puzzled expression on her face. Nurse Sue saw her and asked, "Mrs. Brown, what are you doing up at this hour?" She stared for a moment and then quietly asked, "Can you tell me where I live?"

Nurse Sue took Millie to the day room and handed her a cup of coffee. Trying to start a conversation she asked, "Do you think it's going to snow?" "Oh, I hope not," Millie replied. "Some of my children will be absent today if it does snow." Nurse Sue, remembering Millie had been a schoolteacher gently asked, "How many children in your room, Mrs. Brown?"

A bright smile animated her wrinkled face as if suddenly she were somewhere else, in a springtime when life was new and hope was eternal. "Well, I have twenty-two in my room . . . " And she began to count . . . "sixteen, seventeen, eighteen, twenty . . . " Quickly Nurse Sue asked, "What happened to nineteen?" "Oh, he's absent today." Then Millie paused. "I just can't wait to retire and spend more time with Tom and our grandchildren . . . but I will miss my students . . . " and her voice trailed off into a hundred years ago. "You know . . . those children gave me a reason for living."

For a brief, shining moment their relationship was different. No longer nurse and patient. Now, neighbors having a morning chat over coffee. After a while, Millie's eyes grew heavy with sleep, and Nurse Sue led her back to her room, tucked her in bed, and turned off the light. At 6 A.M. Nurse Sue, on her rounds, returned to give Mrs. Brown her morning medication.

Paul and Silas, in the innermost cells of a Philippian prison, their feet fastened in stocks, began to sing hymns—songs at midnight. Who knows what they sang. Perhaps, Psalm 116 which begins "I love the Lord, because he has heard my voice . . . ; or Psalm 118, "O give thanks to the Lord, for he is good." But the prisoners listened . . . and for that shining moment things were different.

In the bleak midwinter, a nurse and an elderly woman sang their own songs of faith, one remembering, the other listening. And faith lived.

Friend of every old person, You are the One to whom we cry in the darkness of night. You stay with us. You listen, and our faith lives on. Amen.

30

Read Genesis 18:1-15

So Sarah laughed to herself . . . The LORD said to Abraham, "Why did Sarah laugh . . . ?" Sarah denied, saying, "I did not laugh;" for she was afraid. He said, "Oh yes, you did laugh."

Genesis 18:12, 13, 14

Those Who Laugh . . . Last!

When Sarah heard the preposterous news that she would have a child in her old age, she laughed. In fact, she laughed so hard that her sides ached and tears poured down her face. Sarah laughed herself into history, and the child of promise was named Isaac which means "laughter."

Ed Loper tells how he once used the story of Abraham and Sarah for a Bible study in a nursing home. Ed asked one woman what she would think if somebody told her she was pregnant now, today. She replied, "You must be kidding," and started to laugh, a Sarah kind of laugh.

David B. Oliver writes, "One of the last places people expect to experience humor is in a nursing home. For years now, however, I have wanted to write a book on nothing but the humor found there. Every day produces something new. . . . Ask anyone who works in a nursing home about some of the funniest things that have happened during the course of their work, and they will keep you rolling on the floor."

What about the time Mary lost her teeth, and she went to every room on her hall, exchanging teeth. No wonder everyone on the hall had trouble eating the next day! Or what about the time the minister visited Sue on her 100th birthday, and she told him, "Thanks for coming, but I'd be just as glad if you hadn't." Or the time the guest minister spoke too long at chapel, and he said he had enjoyed his visit and would like to come back. "I hope not," said one disgruntled lady. Or what about the time the preacher visited Mrs. Green, and she looked right at him and said, "I sure like our preacher, but I wish he could visit me more!" Almost speechless, the minister replied, "Well, when I see him, I'll tell him to do that."

Even the worst scenarios of aging can be redeemed by a saving sense of humor. Not the "sick jokes" that poke fun at older people; but healthy humor like the kind that made Sarah laugh. After all, we don't stop laughing because we get old, we get old when we stop laughing.

Lord, help me to get a few laughs today.
Amen. 🌫

31

Be angry but do not sin; do not let the sun go down on your anger.

Ephesians 4:26

Good and Mad

He looked at the calendar pasted to the wall with masking tape, covering his tiny space with scenes from afar. "What does time mean when routine controls my life? Why be reminded of mountains and oceans I will never see again?" So in a fit of rage he ripped the calendar from the wall.

She was angry at the way some of the nursing assistants treated the residents. They showed little compassion, displayed no interest in these "old" people, and talked about how they could make more money working at Hardees. She chafed at the thought that some of these care-givers were only interested in their paychecks and had little concern for the residents.

Paul wrote, "Be angry, but do not sin." Too much of our anger is self-centered, focused on our needs. It is a response to things that we perceive keep us from having our own way. We can understand the anger of the man who tore the calendar from his wall. He was angry at the way old age had limited his life and turned its control over to other people.

Moses was angry when he came down from the mountain carrying the sacred tablets of the law, and found the people dancing and singing praises to a golden calf. Moses was angry because the people were misrepresenting God. They worshiped the false, the glittery, the visible, the familiar.

Jesus' anger is evident when he cleansed the temple. Incensed and irate, he turned over the tables and whipped the moneychangers. Jesus' anger was directed at those who had misrepresented God, who had turned the Father's house of prayer into a den of robbers. But Jesus was also angry because the system of courts mistreated people, keeping Gentiles and women out of direct access to God.

The anger of Jesus and Moses is other-directed. Wherever people are mistreated, whenever their well-being is denied, we should be angry. Anger need not lead to resentment or envy, self-assertion or aggressiveness. Christianity asserts that anger can be transformed, through faith, into works of love. Christians need to be *good* and mad and allow that anger to cause constructive change.

Christ, you showed anger when people were mistreated. Help us to be sensitive to that same scene and to be agents of creative change. Amen. ᗌ

32

But Moses' hands grew weary; so they took a stone and put it under him, and he sat on it. Aaron and Hur held up his hands, one on one side, and the other on the other side; so his hands were steady until the sun set.

Exodus 17:12

Sustaining Prayer

The story of the conflict between Joshua and the Amalekites clearly shows the power of an old person's prayer. In the fluctuations of that battle, the key to victory was not in the hands of Joshua and his army battling in the valley, but in those of Moses and Aaron and Hur—all octogenarians—on the mountaintop. As long as Moses held aloft his staff, the battle swayed in favor of Israel. But when from sheer weariness he allowed it to fall, the enemy prevailed.

Moses' arms grew weary, and when he could no longer stand, he sat. When he could no longer hold his hands up, Aaron and Hur, on either side, held them aloft until the victory was won. The tide of the battle in the valley depended not so much on the military prowess of Joshua and his warriors, as it did on the prayers of three old men on the mountaintop. And when the leader, Moses, grew weary, it was Aaron and Hur who held up his arms so that prayers could continue.

We also can be powerful weapons for God's kingdom through intercessory prayer. Cora was one such prayer warrior. She was in her nineties, her vision gone, and her life confined to one room. She often wished she could be more active in the life of her church. On one occasion, she told me that she prayed daily for every member of her church by name. She told me that when she learned the church was struggling through a difficult time with a building program, her prayers intensified. Are we to believe that the ultimate success of that campaign was somehow related to Cora's prayer? I certainly think so.

The Book of James says it well, "Pray for one another, . . . The prayer of the righteous is powerful and effective" (James 5:16). Imagine what a powerful source of spiritual energy might reside in nursing homes, if each person would pray for the church?

Even though we may not be physically in our church, our prayers can keep the church's life revitalized and reenergized.

> *Sweet hour of prayer!*
> *sweet hour of prayer!*
> *that calls me from a world of care,*
> *and bids me at my Father's throne*
> *make all my wants and wishes known.* ☙

Who knows? Perhaps you have come to royal dignity for just such a time as this.

Esther 4:14

———————— ✿ ————————

When Harry Met Sally . . . Again

You'd have to admit it was a strangely different kind of beauty contest. The nine contestants' ages ranged from eighty-seven to a hundred. All, regally dressed for the occasion, entered the decorated room in wheelchairs. Several had not been out of their beds for months. But all were contestants for the "Miss Grace Heights Beauty Queen."

Sitting there, moved by their ageless beauty, I remembered another beauty contest from holy history. When Queen Vashti was deposed, King Ahasuerus ordered a beauty contest in Persia to find his new queen. Urged on by Mordecai, Esther the Jewess, won the favor of the king and became his queen.

One of our contestants, Sally, reminded me of Esther. At age ninety-two, her body was frail, but her spirit and mind were vibrant and well. She did not win the contest, but she was cherished and loved by all for her quick wit and friendly smile.

Harry, also ninety-two, had not seen Sally for years. Longtime friends, their relationship had been broken by the ravages of age. But that night I took Harry to the Grace Heights Beauty Contest to see Sally. They hugged each other as time stood still. The clock had ticked away the years and had taken its toll on their bodies, but nothing had dimmed or destroyed their friendship. They talked of former days and clung to old memories when life was freer and kinder. Then they said goodbye, no doubt for the last time. Sally said, "Come and see me again, Harry. I'm always at home." A hug became their farewell.

Unlike Esther, Sally had not won the beauty contest. Like Esther, she had come "to royal dignity for such a time as this." For one, brief, memorable moment friends were restored to former days, and the past became the present. As Harry entered his room in another health care center, you could sense his happiness. He had seen his old friend. Harry had met Sally once again.

Friend of us all, we thank you that even in our later years when we are weak and heavy laden, you intrude into our lonely hours with a touch of hope. We see a friend we haven't seen for years; we feel renewed, alive again. But you, dear God, never leave us; you are our constant Friend. Amen. 🕊

See! The winter is past; the rains are over and gone. Flowers appear on the earth; the season of singing has come.
Song of Songs 2:11-12 (NIV)

Above the Frost Line

Winter is a difficult time for residents in a nursing home. The Christmas carolers have come and gone; springtime seems forever in the future. The days are short, the nights are long, frost and snow cover the earth, and dismal darkness seems to be everywhere.

Winter is a hard time for residents in a nursing home. They wile away the hours doing nothing—watching television, staring out those endless windows, playing mindless games to kill the time. Not able to go outside or even to sit on the porch, they sit in hallways or in their rooms, hoping someone will come and visit them. But the holiday visitors have gone, and it seems as if no one remembers them.

We gathered in the activity room to sing old songs. Mrs. Bartlett was always there. Now past ninety-five, a victim of Alzheimer's, she babbled on with her nonsense and looked out of eyes that stared holes into your soul. The group wasn't in the mood to sing that gray afternoon as icy rain fell on the frozen ground. They seemed as frozen as that ground. One by one, we sang their songs, old gospel songs they had learned from childhood.

Suddenly, as we were singing "Blessed Assurance," I glanced at Mrs. Bartlett. She smiled at me, and those aged lips began to sing the words,

> Blessed assurance, Jesus is mine!
> O what a foretaste of glory divine!
> Heir of salvation, purchase of God,
>   born of his spirit, washed in
>   his blood.

I couldn't believe it! I took her hand, and we sang together the refrain,

This is my story, this is my song,
  praising my Savior all the day long;
this is my story, this is my song,
  praising my Savior all the day long.

And then she lapsed once again into a language no one understood. But for one brief, radiant moment, she had remembered, in the midst of winter—there was spring. Above the frost line there was hope. Flowers had appeared on the earth; the season of singing had come.

Caring God, we give thanks that when our lives seem cold and meaningless, our hearts can rise above the winter frost to be warmed again by your love. And seasons of singing can come. Amen.

VI. When the Owl Calls Your Name

The life narratives of some nursing home residents highlight worry, disappointment, and
thoughts of death . . .
The mere mention of such common life
themes as family and home unleashes
sobs and expressions of how it may
soon come to an end.

Jaber F. Gubrium

On the seventh day the child died. And the servants of David were afraid to tell him that the child was dead.

2 Samuel 12:18

Why Don't They Tell Us?

Sarah seemed puzzled at Margaret's absence. She was not at her usual place in the dining room, and when Sarah wheeled to her room, her bed was empty. When she asked a nursing assistant, she was told that Margaret had died several days ago. "Why don't they tell us when someone dies?" Sarah exclaimed. "We have a right to know."

The servants of David were afraid to tell the king that his child had died. Granted, their reasons may seem valid, for they said, "He may do himself some harm" (2 Sam. 12:18). But when David heard them whispering together, he knew his child had died. So he rose and ate.

He told his servants, "Now he is dead; why should I fast? Can I bring him back again? I shall go to him, but he will not return to me" (12:22-23). Marvelous picture of honest grief.

It is sad that all too often nursing home personnel maintain almost a conspiracy of silence about a resident's death. Even in a place where death comes weekly, the dead are rushed out to funeral homes, and little is said to other residents. It seems in Western culture we still hide death.

Denying residents the right to know when others die blocks their grief process. As Shakespeare wrote, "He who lacks time to mourn, lacks time to mend." Residents need to know so they can express grief. Furthermore, others' deaths remind us of our own. As John Donne wrote, ". . . any man's death diminishes me, because I am involved in mankind." In a place where death is a reality, it is crucial that residents have the opportunity to work through the awareness of their own death.

Due to the concern of some residents and the chaplain, steps were taken to share the deaths of residents. A memorial table named those who had died in the past month. A memorial service (open to both staff and residents) eulogized those who had died the past month, and gave opportunity for expression of thanksgiving for the lives of those who had died.

Sarah was right. Residents have a right to know when others die. They do not need to be shielded from reality.

Dear God, we want to know when our friends die. We want to grieve their loss and celebrate their victory. We want to remember them . . . and give thanks. Help our caretakers allow us to do that. Amen.

So Rachel died, and she was buried on the way to Ephrath (that is, Bethlehem), and Jacob set up a pillar at her grave.

Genesis 35:19-20

Strength to Journey On

Jacob loved Rachel! She was the joy of his life. He worked and waited fourteen years before her father, Laban, gave his consent for her marriage. After his midnight conversion experience at Peniel (Gen. 32) and return to Canaan, Jacob experienced many difficulties. He had become lame at Peniel and remained so for the rest of his life (Gen. 32:21-32). His daughter, Dinah, was raped by a foreigner (Gen. 34). Some of his sons married foreign wives. Then Rebekah's nurse, Deborah died (Gen. 35:8). But nothing was as devastating to him as the death of his wife Rachel.

Rachel died in childbirth in Bethlehem. So Jacob buried her outside the town of Bethlehem and set a pillar upon her grave which still is there. His grief was beyond words. But the writer of Genesis says, "Jacob journeyed on, and pitched his tent beyond the tower of Eder." Until his death he would grieve Rachel's loss. Yet, Jacob journeyed on.

Life went on. He had a family to care for, and beyond his family the larger family of Israel. Other lives needed Jacob, and God needed him to keep the biblical story moving.

Elizabeth Moreland Jones also experienced the loss of a spouse; her husband, Harry, died after open heart surgery. In her book *Not One Bird Stopped Singing* Elizabeth vividly describes her painful loss: "The death of a much-loved spouse calls into question all the certainties of life and faith. What has once been a given is no more. . . . The dreary details of death drag on, consuming energy without bringing comfort." Yet, her understanding of grief and her Christian faith helped her find the resilience of the bird who never stops singing.

As older people, we suffer many losses, but none is harder than the loss of a spouse.

Scott Sullender says it well: "The loss of a spouse is one of the hardest losses to let go of . . . we must again let go . . . let go again, knowing that the invisible arms of the Almighty will support us and carry us forward to a new stage of our journey called life." Some older people never seem to recover from the loss of a spouse. Their final days are spent in prolonged grief. Others, like Jacob, journey on and find new beginnings.

Loving God, when we lose our spouse, it seems as if we have lost ourselves. We feel that our only happiness lies in cherishing their memory, not in a new life in the future. Help us through these dark and difficult days. Amen.

Then Jesus went with them to a place called Gethsemane. . . . He took with him Peter and the two sons of Zebedee, and began to be grieved and agitated. Then he said to them, "I am deeply grieved, even to death; remain here, and stay awake with me."

Matthew 26:36-38

My Greatest Fear

Sitting in his darkened room, Sam wanted to talk about death. His best friend had died just yesterday, and even in a place where death occurs as a silenced, hushed event, it was on his mind. "It's not something that most people talk about here," he said, "but I'm not afraid to admit I am afraid."

"What is it about death that makes you afraid?" I asked. "The dying part," he replied. "What about the dying part?" I asked. "The part about dying alone," he replied.

When Jesus faced his imminent death in the Garden of Gethsemane, he took Peter, James, and John with him so he would not be alone. He asked them to "remain . . . and stay awake," for he was deeply grieved, even unto death. The full brunt of what the cup would cost him on the morrow filled his consciousness for he realized that on the cross he would bear the whole human tragedy. Jesus needed the presence of his friends at that moment.

Older people feel deeply the deaths of others. Karl Rahner writes,

> When I look back in this way, I see my life as a long highway filled by a column of marching men. Every moment someone breaks out of the line and goes off silently, without a word or wave of farewell . . . The number of marchers gets steadily smaller, for the new men coming up to fill the ranks are really not marching in my column at all.

In a nursing home, almost every week someone breaks out of line and goes off silently without a word or wave of farewell.

But their deaths do cause others to be worried about their own dying. Listening to residents tell their stories, one always hears thoughts of death. When they talk about family or home, they know all that will soon come to an end.

But their greatest worry is dying alone. If Jesus, the Son of God, needed friends present when he faced the reality of his own death, then it is a human need for us too. I assured Sam he would not die alone. When that time came, I would be there with him. That seemed to calm his fears. He never mentioned it again, but when he died, I was there for support—as a friend.

Saviour Christ, you needed friends present in your dying hour. But when that hour came, they all left you alone. But your death means we will never be alone when that hour comes for us. Thank you. Amen. ✎

38

And not only that, but we also boast in our sufferings, knowing that suffering produces endurance, and endurance produces character, and character produces hope.
Romans 5:3-4

Suffering Brings Meaning

They had been married for sixty-two years, and for the last five years had lived across the hall from each other in a nursing home. Even though she suffered from Alzheimer's, he was patient and kind with her and attentive to her needs. When she died, he sank into deep despair and refused to speak. There are no words to describe the loneliness and pain of older persons when they lose their life companion. It is life's greatest distress.

I told him the story that I read in Viktor Frankl's book *Man's Search for Meaning*. An elderly doctor was overcome by his wife's death two years earlier. He had loved deeply. Frankl asked him, "What would have happened, Doctor, if you had died first, and your wife would have had to survive you?" "Oh," he said, "for her this would have been terrible; how she would have suffered!" Frankl replied, "You see, Doctor, such a suffering has been spared her, and it was you who have spared her this suffering."

He listened intently and nodded his head without saying a word. I hope he understood. In no way could I diminish his pain or ease his grief. I just prayed that his suffering could bring new meaning to his life.

Wayne Muller reminds us "that whatever sorrow or grief, illness or harm is given us, there is within us a tangible presence, a spirit of God that will bear us up, hold us, and keep us strong. Regardless of how we are hurt, our divine nature will help us bear the weight of it." How true!

The worst pain cannot be strong enough to quench the light within us or the resilience of our spirit. In fact, sorrow does not have to mar our lives; it can be a bridge to great healing. That is why Paul wrote to the Romans that "we can boast in sufferings, since suffering produces character . . ."

During the weeks that ensued, I often visited my friend. He seemed at peace with his loss; on one gray afternoon, he looked at me with those sad, yet discerning eyes that bored into your soul and said, "I'm okay now; time will never heal my hurt; but I'm going on, and I now realize that my loss is my cross." On that bleak midwinter afternoon, I knew that the light of his life had not been extinguished.

Caring God, when we suffer, help us to focus on you, and find that divine nature that helps us bear what seems unbearable pain. Amen.

39

O death, your sentence is welcome to one in want, whose strength is failing, to one worn out with age and a thousand worries, resentful and impatient! Do not dread death's sentence.

*Ecclesiasticus 41:2,3a (NJB)

Death Is Not the Final Word

Jesus must have shocked the professional mourners of his day with his words when he entered the house of Jairus. They were sure Jairus' little daughter was dead, and thus they had already begun their wailing and lamentation. Jesus asked, "Why all this commotion and crying?" He took the child by the hand and spoke the words *Talitha cum,* "Little girl, arise."

---

*Ecclesiasticus is found in the Apocrypha in Protestant translations of the Bible. It is part of the writings between the Testaments.

How did this little bit of Aramaic get itself embedded in the Greek of the gospels? There can be only one reason. Mark got his information from Peter who was there, and he could never forget Jesus' voice. In his mind and memory he could hear *Talitha cum* all his life. The loveliness and gentleness of Jesus' words were engraved on his heart, so much so that he was unable to think of it in Greek at all because his memory could only hear the very words Jesus spoke.

Death in a nursing home is a strange event. Instead of professional mourners, dead persons are whisked away with little announcement to staff or residents. Death is hushed, a silenced event, and residents often guess at what has happened. One lady observed, "The man in room 104 must have died last night because they've got the doors closed today. That's the only time they close the doors during the day."

There is a striking contrast in the gospel story between the despair of the mourners and the hope of Jesus. There is also the contrast between the unrestrained distress of the mourners and the calm serenity of Jesus. The difference lay in Jesus' perfect confidence and trust in God.

When death comes to a nursing home, the contrast would be between the polite silence of the professional caregivers and the faith of the residents. As Jesus Ben Sirach wrote in Ecclesiasticus, "O death, your sentence is welcome . . . to one worn out with age and a thousand worries." Many residents have made their peace with death, and do not dread it.

It is time to practice Jesus' approach to death, end the conspiracy of silence, face death with serenity and acceptance. For Christians, death is not the last word. As one ninety-six-year-old resident said, "They may put dirt over my body, but I'll be in a better world." That's the kind of faith that overcomes death.

Grant us to really know, O Loving God,
that death is swallowed up in victory.
Amen. 🌫

You will come to the grave in full vigor,
like sheaves gathered in season.

　　　　　　　　　　　Job 5:26 NIV

Coming to Harvest

Older persons in nursing homes often become depressed and sad when they look at their present situation. What is there to live for?　It seems as if they merely exist to die, but looking back at life can bring a renewed sense of meaning.

Joyce told her story. Her husband had been killed in a tragic train wreck when he was thirty years old, leaving her with two small daughters. Somehow she managed, working in a cotton mill and doing her best for her girls. Now, she spoke with joy that both her daughters were nurses and had happy family lives. When we told her that her accomplishment was a monument to her faith and courage, she seemed so proud.

No longer sad and downcast, now she told the nursing assistants that her life was a monument, and she showed them pictures of her girls. Some months later, she died; and as Job wrote, she came to the grave in full vigor, "like sheaves gathered in season."

Boyd was another person who "came to the grave in full vigor." He hoed to the end of the row and maintained his sense of humor and grace until death came. At his funeral, the epitaph he wrote for himself was read.

Epitaph

Only a memory
The season's gone.
Summer's green mystery
Winter's bleak song.

Only a memory
The toil and strife
The ambitions and dreams
Of a simple life.

Only a memory
Thoughts, hopes, and fears
Joys and sorrows
Of earthly years.

There in memory
A stone to attest
He sleeps here untroubled
The final rest.

Boyd H. Houser

Ever present Friend, when we know the meaning of our lives we can die with dignity and peace. For that we are grateful. Amen.

Now listen to me, you that say, "Today or tomorrow we will travel to a certain city, where we will stay a year and go into business and make a lot of money." You don't even know what your life tomorrow will be! You are like a puff of smoke, which appears for a moment and then disappears.

James 4:13-14 (TEV)

A Puff of Smoke

We gathered to remember nine residents who had died in the past month. It was a strange congregation with some residents unaware of what was happening and others in a somber mood as they thought of those who had died and of their own death. The light of nine candles reminded us of the lives of these nine who had died. For years the light of their lives had burned brightly. Some persons who were present spoke about how they remembered them, while others spoke about the deceased residents' contributions to the home. In their latter days, their candles had become "dimly burning wicks," and yet flickered with faith and hope.

I spoke briefly about each resident, remembering him or her as I lingered above the light. After the benediction, I extingquished out the candles to symbolize the residents' departure from this life to the next.

Wisps of smoke rose to the ceiling. The silence of the room was broken by a person who exclaimed, "Look! Our lives are like a puff of smoke. We're here and then gone."

The book of James is packed with practical Christianity. It never argues faith against works, but demands a faith that works. The writer reminds us that no one knows what tomorrow may bring, and life, at best, is short.

William Penn, the Quaker leader and founder of Pennsylvania, penned a beautiful prayer for those who had died.

We give back to you, O God, those whom you gave to us. You did not lose them when you gave them to us, and we do not lose them by their return to you. Your dear Son has taught us that life is eternal and love cannot die. So death is only a horizon, and a horizon is only the limit of our sight.

I fail to understand why death must be shielded from residents of nursing homes. Every day they are continually taking leave, saying good-by, looking toward the end. Each person's death reminds them that good-byes are a vital part of their lives.

The memory of that service lingers. The light flickered and was extinguished. The smoke rose and then dissolved. The deafening silence filled the room. What we call death, they saw as the death of death.

Lord, we believe; help our unbelief.
Amen. ☙

VII. Home at Last

The word *home* summons up a place
where you feel you belong
and which in some sense belongs to you,
a place where you feel that all is somehow
ultimately well
even if things aren't going all that well
at any given moment.

Frederick Buechner

42

Now we see in a mirror dimly, but then we will see face to face. Now I know only in part; then I will know fully, even as I have been fully known.

1 Corinthians 13:12

Hope for Mrs. Paper Face

Mary suffered from Alzheimer's disease, often called "the funeral that never ends." She wandered aimlessly in the endless halls of the nursing home, stopping only to ask me, "Can you tell me who I am or where I live?" Gently I took her to her room, and she slumped in an old chair. I noted a faded wedding picture on the mantel of her room.

Mary's face reminded me of the song "Masquerade" from the New Year's party in *Phantom of the Opera*. One line from the song states "paper faces on parade."

I visited her husband who lived across the hall. Sadly, he said, "She has Alzheimer's disease, and it is so hard for me to talk to her anymore; she just doesn't know anything," and his voice trailed off into a cavernous silence. I learned they had been married sixty-four years.

Suddenly Mary appeared, worried about her husband. Her one contact with reality was her love for him. She sat in stony silence in his old chair while we talked.

I noticed a picture on his dresser of a lovely, dark-haired woman. He told me that was her picture when she was twenty-one, a gift for him one month before their marriage. I looked into her hidden face and said, "Why, Mary, who is this lovely young woman? Can this be you? I believe it is." She smiled. One of the most radiant smiles I have ever seen illuminated her face. The masquerade had ended. I saw no paper face, but a face brilliant with light. "Look, look," her husband exclaimed. "She smiled. She understands." She knew who she had been and now was.

Months later Mary died with pneumonia. I read Paul's hymn of love at her memorial service. Those words haunted me: "Now we see in a mirror, dimly, but then we will see face to face. Now I know only in part; then I shall know fully, even as I have been fully known" (1 Cor. 13:12). Her masquerade was finally over. She was face to face with God, and now "was fully known."

Loving Father, like Adam and Eve in the garden, we hide from you and from others our true selves. Give us the hope that one day we can be who we are. Amen.

43 Read Galatians 5:1, 13-15

*For freedom Christ has set us free. Stand
firm, therefore, and do not submit again to
a yoke of slavery.*

Galatians 5:1

Untethered Frances

Do our minds wear out with age or do they
just fill up and overflow? Sometimes I think
that is what has happened to people with
Alzheimer's. Their rich memories of the past
seem to have overflowed into the present.

Frances was tethered to a nursing home
chair. She looked so sad. She would often pull
at the restraints that kept her safe. They kept
her from wandering off and climbing on a city
bus or stepping in front of a car, or worse.

When Frances talked, she was free of all
restraints, even those of time and space. When
she talked, the past was present again. To her I
was no longer the awkward minister who did
not know what to say, but I was whoever she

willed me to be, and the nursing home was no longer her safe prison but whatever she wanted it to be.

At first I tried to restrain her. I tried to tie her to the reality of her present by telling her over and over again who I was and where she was. But her mind could not be tied fast to the present. She refused to be confined to the awkward conversations within the walls of the nursing home. She would not allow it. She would not accept that "reality."

She took me to wonderful places. We went to U.S.O. dances and said good-bye to many handsome young men and one very special young man. We played on her grandfather's farm, ate fresh peaches, swam in the creek, and gathered wild flowers. We rode streetcars to work. We visited India and Africa. We went out into the Richmond city streets on V-E Day.

We would skip through the years and places as quickly as one memory triggered another. We were not even confined to traveling in a straight line. We would go from childhood memory of making fresh peach ice cream to receiving word from the War that her special young man would not be coming home; then back again to the safety of her childhood.

Sometimes she would pause, look around the nursing home, get a puzzled look on her face, and catch a glimpse of reality, but she never stayed long.

"Poor old Frances," people would say. "It is sad what has happened to her mind."

It was sad to see her that way. She would have been embarrassed to see herself tied to the chair. But that was not her reality. She saw herself as she had been at other times in far better places. And as I made friends with her reality, she was not such a sad figure. At times I could almost see the mischievous little girl and the brave young woman. At times I could even thank God for her overflowing memories and the escape they gave her.

Frances is free of all restraints now. I celebrate her freedom. But sometimes I miss our trips.

You have given us freedom within ourselves, despite being bound by circumstance or other constraints. Help us to celebrate that unbridled freedom we see in others . . . and ourselves.
Amen.

44

But Jesus, aware of this, said to them, "Why do you trouble the woman? She has performed a good service for me . . . Truly I tell you, wherever this good news is proclaimed in the whole world, what she has done will be told in remembrance of her."

Matthew 26:10, 13

Breaking Open the Alabaster Jar

Who was the woman who quietly walked into the house of Simon the leper at Bethany and anointed Jesus with that costly ointment? Some believe it was Mary of Bethany; others, Mary Magdalene. Her identity matters little. What matters is her lavish love in breaking open an expensive jar of perfume to anoint Jesus.

It did seem quite a waste, a foolish thing to do. Mark's Gospel says it was worth an entire year's wages. It could have been sold, and so many good and sensible things done with it, especially for the ever-present poor. But she wasted it. Everyone said it was foolish—except Jesus, the only one who really understood her act.

He knew she had seized the moment that would not come again. The cross was near now, the darkness and pain. While there was still time she was anointing Jesus as her king, her Messiah. He saw it as a creative and lovely thing that time would never tarnish.

God wants us to be extravagant in our expression of gratitude. Often this is most lacking in nursing homes. Nursing assistants are often unappreciated and devalued. The burden of their tireless, difficult care of residents could be made lighter by simple expressions of gratitude. When we break open the alabaster box of appreciation we are doing a lovely thing that time will not tarnish.

Was there ever such a seeming extravagant waste as Calvary? Even his enemies were baffled as they cried out, "He saved others; he cannot save himself . . . let him come down from the cross now, and we will believe in him" (Matt. 27:42). Many who saw his precious blood poured out like wine must have wondered, "Why this waste?" But this was God's master stroke, his extravagant gift of love to a world wasted by sin.

In response to God's lavish love we are called to show love and appreciation as we break open our alabaster jars of precious perfume.

> Were the whole realm of nature mine,
> that were an offering far too small;
> love so amazing, so divine,
> demands my soul, my life, my all.

Creative God, help me to crack open the box of my self-contained appreciation and show love to someone today.
Amen.

45

Read Luke 16:19-31

So then, whenever we have an opportunity, let us work for the good of all, and especially those of the family of faith.
Galatians 6:10

Serving from Wheelchairs

We had been studying the parables of Jesus in our Bible study group, and we discussed the story of Lazarus. I thought the group would identify with the poor man Lazarus, who lay helpless day after day at the gate of the rich man, begging for crumbs. These were people totally dependent on others for simple things.

I felt awkward talking about this story, for how could these people serve others, confined to wheelchairs, so much in need of help themselves. But the discussion took a strange twist. Instead of Lazarus, they seemed to zero in on the rich man, lamenting his neglect of the poor.

One lady exclaimed, "You know, there are some things you do in life which won't put you in jail, but you could end up in hell." Another remarked, "The rich man did nothing wrong. He just didn't see the beggar at his gate."

Conversation shifted to their time and place. I asked them how they could serve others in this place. One woman said she cared for her roommate who was deaf and became her "ears." Another said she liked to sew afghans for other residents. A third, a World War II veteran, said, "I still stand guard duty in the hall, and if anyone is having problems, I tell the nurses." A former nurse said she always looked for opportunities to feed other residents who could not feed themselves.

Almost everyone had already been serving others in quiet, unobtrusive ways. Finally, Lilly, a dear lady who never moved from her wheelchair, said, "Only last week I helped Marie get a glass of water." Christ's timeless word about the value of a cup of cold water (Matt. 10:42) came alive in that moment.

Strange, isn't it? How God confounds the wisdom of the world and makes reality known through simple people. I recalled Jesus' prayer, "I thank you, Father . . . because you have hidden these things from the wise and the intelligent and have revealed them to infants" (Matt. 11:25). These saints in wheelchairs resembled the simple, single-hearted little children. They did serve from wheelchairs!

Help me, dear Lord, to brighten the corner where I am. Amen. 𝒞𝒷

And [Anna] was a widow of about eighty-four years, who did not depart from the temple, but served God with fastings and prayers night and day.

Luke 2:37 (NKJV)

A Christmas Presence

The carolers had come and gone, but their music lingered. Everyone seemed to join in the conversation that followed their departure. Sam said that he always thought that the wise men brought gifts of gold, frankincense, and *mirth*, and it seemed a joyous time. Residents who usually sat in silence had mumbled the words of the carols. But their message of peace and joy sounded like brass to Anna. Her husband had been dead for four months, and nothing seemed to ease her pain or fill the gap in her heart. She and Charlie had lived together for sixty-two years, and no Christmas peace could fill the hole in her life.

"We had so looked forward to these last years together," she told her nurse. "Everyone said we were the perfect late life couple. But he's gone, and Christmas just won't seem the same without him." She went on, "I know those church people mean well; but don't they realize how sad it makes us feel when they sing those songs?" Her voice trailed off as she wheeled herself back to her darkened room.

As was her custom, she turned to her old, battered, well-used Bible that has been her constant companion throughout life. "I'll read the Christmas story again," she softly said to herself. "It seems new every time I read it." She read Luke's account of the shepherds and their visit to the manger, and then she continued reading that second chapter of Luke.

When she read the story of Anna, she paused. "I never knew Anna had been a widow for so long and that she was so devoted to God." Like Mary, who pondered the birth stories in her heart, she savored each one. "But Anna—what a wonderful model for me now." A strange new Presence seemed to fill her heart. The Christ who had been born in

Bethlehem had been born again in an old widow's heart in a lonely nursing home outside town.

Once again she heard lingering strains of the carolers as they strolled down endless halls. They were singing a carol she had never heard before. She listened intently.

> What can I give him poor as I am?
> If I were a shepherd,
>   I would bring a lamb;
> if I were a Wise Man,
>   I would do my part;
> yet what can I give him?
> give my heart.
>
> Christina G. Rossetti

And those aged, wrinkled hands were folded in prayer.

Dear Father, help me at Christmas, as you did Anna, to find the Christ child in my heart. In my loss, may that be my gain. Amen.

How lovely is your dwelling place, O Lord of hosts! . . . Even the sparrow finds a home, and the swallow a nest for herself, where she may lay her young, at your altars, O Lord of hosts.

Psalm 84:1, 3

Everyone Needs a Staying Place

The writer of Psalm 84 is expressing his joy at finding a home in the temple of Yahweh. He noticed that a little sparrow, that ubiquitous bird that flies everywhere and settles nowhere, had made a nest in the Temple. Like the sparrow, the psalmist also had found a staying place in the house of God.

Each of us has an empty place in our hearts that is in the shape of God; and that means nothing or no one can entirely or ultimately fill it. Try as we will to fill that place with other things, sooner or later they will leave us unsatisfied. We are never really "at home" here as we long for a home we have never seen and cannot easily imagine.

While it is true that we are always pilgrims and sojourners in this world and heaven is our true home, we still need a staying place. One resident in the nursing home expressed it well, "I know all that people expect me to do is sit around and wait to die. They keep telling me heaven is my home. But while I'm still on this earth, I need a staying place."

Going to a nursing home is a major transition. It is in-between-time. Paul Tournier describes this between-time in these words: "So there is always in life a place to leave, and a new place to find, and in between a zone of hesitation and uncertainty tinged with more or less intense anxiety."

An inspector was surveying a nursing home. A resident shared some of her concerns. In an humble way she said that nursing assistants did not answer her call bell or wake her up to take her medicine. She found it difficult to sleep at night because of the noisy caregivers. The inspector said, "You must share that with the proper authorities. Remember, they work here; *this is your home.*"

Granted, we will never be really at home here. Our true home is with God, and our hearts are restless until they rest in God. It is at Bethlehem where God was homeless, that we most feel at home. But, in the spirit of the One who made his home in our history, we pray that every person in a nursing home will hear the words, *"This is your home."*

O Loving Jesus, you had no place to lay your head, but you endured homelessness for us, that we might be at home with you. Thanks be to God. Amen.

*Do not lose your fearlessness now, then,
since the reward is so great. You will need
perseverance if you are to do God's will
and gain what he has promised . . .
We are not the sort of people who* draw
back, *and are lost by it; we are the sort who
keep our* faith *until our souls are saved.*

Hebrews 10:36, 39 (NJB)

Two Old Women

The book was worn from use; its cover was
tattered and torn. Since Lottie had brought the
book to the nursing home, it has passed from
room to room, through many hands of older
women. The favorite book was *Two Old
Women.*

In this book Velma Wallis tells the story of
two elderly Native American women abandoned by a migrating tribe that faced
starvation brought on by the harsh Arctic

weather and a shortage of fish and game. Their names were Ch'idzigyaak (named because she reminded her parents of a chickadee bird when she was born) and Sa' (meaning star because her mother had been looking at the fall night sky).

Abandoned to die by their own people, Sa' says to Ch'idzigyaak, "My friend, . . . We can sit here and wait to die. We will not have long to wait . . . they have condemned us to die! They think that we are old and useless. They forget that we too have earned the right to live! So I say, if we are going to die, my friend, let us die trying, not sitting."

The story tells how these two women did survive and even found food to share with other members of the tribe. After being reunited with the tribe, the chief appointed the two women to honorary positions within the tribe. The people made a promise never again to abandon their elders. Betrayal ended in new respect for elders. The two women's persistent courage and willingness to "die trying" not only helped them survive but brought new hope for all the elderly of the Gwich'in People who lived on the upper Yukon River in Alaska.

Why has this story captivated so many residents of the nursing home? Perhaps because it tells of how we can survive in the bleakest of situations when we are tempted to give up and surrender to despair. Like Sa' and Ch'idzigyaak, we can decide not to give up but "die trying" and keep the faith until life ends. As the writer to the Hebrews said so well, "We are not the sort of people who *draw back* . . . ; we are the sort who keep our *faith* until our souls are saved."

For those brave women and men who do not give up when life tumbles in, we give you thanks, O Lord, and praise them for their stubborn courage and resolute faith. Amen. 🐬

49 Read Philippians 4:4-8

A cheerful heart is good medicine, but a crushed spirit dries up the bones.

Proverbs 17:22 (NIV)

The Clown of Grace Manor

Old Robert was such a clown! He was always joking with the caregivers and teasing the women. At age ninety-six, he had outlived three wives and liked to terrify the women residents with his claim he was looking for number four. Whenever a group met, Robert's saving sense of humor kept us all in stitches. We called him "The Clown of Grace Manor."

We all remember the Halloween party when he put on his clown costume, wearing that red wig and synthetic lavender hair. He roamed the halls bursting into laughter every now and then—sometimes for reasons he only knew. But we loved him for it. Then old age and cancer struck him a mortal blow, but even then he laughed and said, "Guess soon they'll be covering this old carcass of mine with dirt, but I won't be there. God will give me the last laugh."

Laughter is good medicine. It is especially therapeutic for older people whose lives may be terribly grim. It helps the immune system by relieving stress. No wonder ancient kings had court jesters who eased tension with comic relief. Robert helped us all get a lot of smileage out of life.

Frederick Buechner tells the story of Lyman Woodard, the "clown in the belfry." When the church dedicated a new steeple with a bell in it, Lyman stood on his head in the belfry with his feet toward heaven. Buechner tells us, "Let us never forget Lyman Woodard either, silhouetted up there against the blue Rupert sky. Let us join him in the belfry with our feet toward Heaven like his, because Heaven is where we are heading. That is our faith and what better image of faith could there be?"

Let us not forget Robert's gift of humor either. His room now is still. Robert is gone to that wondrous, blessed land of eternal joy.

That was made possible when God played the ultimate joke on the devil and raised Jesus on the third day!

Every now and then when we gather as a group or eat together in the dining room, we can still hear his laughter. He was such a clown and his laughter has never died.

Teach us, Joyous God, that we can rejoice when life mighty near ruins us. Teach us, Christ of Joy, that pain and joy are not strangers. Amen. 🐾

When they had come to the land of Canaan, Abram passed through the land to the place at Shechem, to the oak of Moreh. . . . So he built there an altar unto the LORD.

Genesis 12:5-6, 7

Home at Last

Abraham was called by God to leave his home, the fully developed urban civilization of Ur of the Chaldees. He takes up again the nomadic life of his forebears and journeys to Canaan. When he settled in the land, he built an altar to the Lord, and bought a field, the field of Ephron, so he might have a place to bury his wife.

To use Martin Buber's phrase, there is a vast difference between the "I-It" place and the "I-Thou" place. Anyone can build a house, but only God can create a home. No wonder, then, that Abraham first built an altar on his arrival in Canaan. As the psalmist wrote, "Unless the LORD builds the house, those who build it labor in vain" (Psalm 127:1).

Feeling "at home" in a nursing home takes time and prayer. Lea Pardue wrote in a past issue of *Journal of Religious Gerontology*, "Eventually this recoil stage develops in reorganization. Reorganization represents spiritual well-being. . . . The resident can finally affirm life in relationship to God, self, community . . . The time of crisis has ended, and the resident feels comfortable in involvement with the community."

For some residents, however, life becomes a constant homesickness for their former home. They never seem to realize that they can't go home again. They end their days in sadness and pain. For others, they now realize where they live is their home. This will ordinarily be the last home where they live. They welcome visitor but not intruders. They enjoy activities but not silly games. Home should not simply be "the place that when you have to go there, they have to take you in." It should also be a place where you can feel comfortable with yourself and others.

Koheleth referred to life after death as going home. "Man goes to his eternal home" (Eccles. 12:5, NIV). That is the final journey of life, but until that moment, wherever we are needs to be our home.

Merciful God, we do miss our homes, but help us to make this place our home now. Amen. ∽

All of these died in faith without having received the promises, but from a distance they saw and greeted them. They confessed that they were strangers and foreigners on the earth.

Hebrews 11:13

Something Is Always Missing . . . Until

Frederick Buechner in his novel *Treasure Hunt* tells about the homecoming of Antonio Parr. On his return home Antonio finds that his small son and some other children have a sign for him that reads WELCOME HONE, with the last line of the M in home missing so that it turns into an N. Buechner wisely says that it is significant of the fact that there is always something missing from our homes here. We are always strangers and foreigners on this earth.

This is the ringing truth of the eleventh chapter of Hebrews in which the writer talks about the heroes and heroines of the faith who were never fully "at home" on this earth, for they "desired a better country, a heavenly one." Settling in on this earth was not the last journey, for they looked for the true homeland.

The prophet Jeremiah saw a day when God would "bring them from the land of the north, and gather them from the farthest parts of the earth" (Jer. 31:8). Jeremiah points toward the future, toward the day when all of God's creation will gather to sit at a table in the kingdom of God. He pictures the refugees' homecoming, not marching but limping. It is a powerful picture of home—the home toward which we all stagger, the table around which the circle will never again be broken.

It is incorrect to say that everyone who goes to a nursing home goes there to wait to die. For many life goes on in amazing ways, and this does become their home. They need to be reminded of Paul's words that "if (when) the earthly tent we live in is destroyed, we have a building from God, an eternal house in heaven, not built by human hands" (2 Cor. 5:1, NIV).

In *The Longing for Home* Buechner is right that the home we long for and belong to "is finally a kingdom which exists both within us and among us as we wend our prodigal ways through the world in search of it." Wherever we are, we can find a home within the wilderness, but we will never find that perfect home until God calls us home.

Loving God, thank you for putting eternity in our hearts, so that we are never completely at home here but wait our place in the Father's house with many rooms. Amen. ℘

52

Then Jacob called his sons, and said: "Gather around, that I may tell you what will happen to you in days to come."

Genesis 49:1

Never Too Old to Learn from Our Elders

Living or working in a nursing home is a never ending learning experience. Being with older people means their lives are acknowledged, and ours are enriched. They are our wisdom teachers. And how much we need their wisdom when we remember we spend only a quarter of our lives growing up and then three quarters of them growing old.

Jacob never went to a nursing home, but late in his life, when he lay on his death bed, he assembled his sons around him. In each instance, Jacob predicted the future of his son and his successors. His insight into what the future might bring was valued wisdom for those who became the originators of the twelve tribes of Israel.

Joel S. Savinshinsky concludes his lively account of life in an American nursing home with these words:

> While the frail elderly show us only one of the possible fates that await us, many of the experiences that they and their caregivers go through are common to each of us. These include the need to deal with loss; the desire to create a meaningful account of our lives; and the struggle to bridge the gaps between expectation and reality. The old and those who are for them can teach us about ourselves if we are willing to listen to them, to consider their questions—and when necessary— to respect their silence.

Yes, the frail elderly are our teachers. We need to drink of the fountains of wisdom which flow from those who have learned to live by living, whose halting steps are marks indicating that they have been through enough battles to know what the warfare of life is all about.

Our Native American friends call the aged "wisdom keepers." So they are, and as we enter the cusp of a new century, we need the wisdom which radiates from the lives of those who have long journeyed the well-traveled roads and who know from experience the perils and pitfalls on the way.

But more than wisdom, we can find faith in the residents of nursing homes. As we hold their gnarled and wrinkled hands, or hug their necks, or sit with them in their rooms, we know we are in the presence of faith, "the assurance of things hoped for, the conviction of things not seen."

We visited a retired minister who suffered more losses from old age than could be mentioned. Yet he reminisced with us, told a few jokes, and gave us his blessing. As we left, my friend said, "He is still a spiritual giant; you could see it in his eyes."

Help us to find the meaning of faith in the face of an aged person today. Amen.

53

Love is patient; love is kind . . . . It does not insist on its own way; it is not irritable or resentful; . . . It bears all things, believes all things, hopes all things, endures all things. Love never ends.

1 Corinthians 13:4, 5, 7-8

Love Breaks through the Garble

Mrs. Jones, age ninety-six, suffers from Alzheimer's and sits endlessly in her wheelchair, clutching her stuffed animals. I try in vain to understand her senseless garble. It is like the old radio transmissions when the signal is weak or unclear or filled with extraneous static. I look into her old eyes and wonder if she ever understands.

When David Dodson Gray's mother, suffering from Alzheimer's, entered a nursing home, he began writing distant family members about his daily visits with her. David fed her and told her the latest family stories and political events. He describes learning how "to listen to garble," when at times a few words and sentence fragments come clear. He learned that whatever his mother is telling him, "though garbled, is still rational, still coherent, still a reference of the same reality we have always loved and shared together." The most difficult skill was "talking to garble, . . . in such a way as to allow, or even encourage, my mother to make the effort to communicate with me."

Two and a half years after his mother's death, David put his letters together in the form of a book, *I Want to Remember: A Son's Reflection on His Mother's Alzheimer Journey*. He wrote, "There is much I regret about the disease and what a wasting it was of her in those years. But I am grateful too for the use we made of that time, salvaging so much even while we were both losing so much."

Surely this is a classic example of what Paul meant by *agapé* love, which "bears all things, believes all things, hopes all things, endures all things." David showed that love for his mother, paying careful attention to her garble, taking their communication seriously.

One afternoon, I tried to talk to Mrs. Jones. I picked up a clue from the smile on her face when I mentioned how she used to sing in the church choir. I droned on, and finally, to my amazement, in a soft, sure voice, she said, "Thank you for coming," as clear as a bell. It was an incredible grace moment for both of us.

Friend of the confused, Saviour of the lost, Comforter of the hopeless, you never leave us or forsake us. Amen. ☙

At evening time there shall be light.
Zechariah 14:7

Faces to the Evening Sun

We had gathered for a late afternoon vesper service. The residents lined up in their wheelchairs or ambled into the room, pushing their walkers. Just then the evening sun shone through the windows and lit the room with a warm light.

No doubt old age is an introduction to death. Yet, as Joseph Folliet says in *The Evening Sun, Growing Old Beautifully*, "But what is forgotten so easily is that the evening of life can also be the evening sun and that it contains both a promise and a consolation. We forget that the evening sun can be just as beautiful as the sun that shines in the early morning or at midday and sometimes even more beautiful . . . it also assures us that the light and heat do not die . . . At the end of the night, a new sun is shining."

The aged Zechariah, a priest in the temple, was struck speechless for months because he did not believe the message of the angel that he and Elizabeth would have a son. But when John was born he was filled with the Holy Spirit and spoke these words, "By the tender mercy of our God, the dawn from on high will break upon us, to give light to those who sit in darkness and in the shadow of death, to guide our feet into the way of peace" (Luke 1:78-79). In the evening of his life, there was a new light.

One of the residents, a former artist, commented, "We need some sunflowers in this room. They are flowers that are always turned toward the sun, toward the light." Sitting in that chapel, watching those faces turned toward the evening sun, I was reminded of sunflowers. Some of those sitting there would soon face that final night when death's shadow would fall across their lives. But the evening sun was there, and in a better world their faces would be turned toward the eternal light.

We closed by singing the hymn, "Sun of My Soul," and the evening sun reminded us of Christ, the Son of God.

Sun of my soul! Thou Saviour dear,
It is not night if Thou be near;
Oh, may no earthborn cloud arise
To hide Thee from Thy servant's eyes!

One elderly gentleman said, "This is holy ground. It seems as if Christ himself is here. In a dark place, some love is found." Faces to the evening sun . . . and "at evening there was light."

O Lord, support us all the day long, until the shadows lengthen and the evening comes, and the busy world is hushed, and the fever of life is over, and our work is done. Then in your mercy grant us a safe lodging, and a holy rest, and peace at the last. Amen. ✍

John Henry Newman

Appendix

A Room Blessing
for a New Resident

RESIDENT/LEADER: We are here to welcome a new friend, _____, into _____ and to ask God's blessing upon this room prepared for her/his use. We know that "unless the Lord build the house, they labor in vain that build it," and no place can be home without God's presence.

ADMINISTRATOR/MINISTER: We are here to reassure you that God is present with you as you live in this room. God is your refuge and strength . . . your ever present help. We remember how the psalmist found that a sparrow found a home at the altar of God. So, we know you will find a home in this room and with us in this place.

LET US PRAY: *(Resident reads prayer with visitors if he/she is able to do so.)* **Father in Heaven, you have set the solitary in families, and we ask now that you make your servant feel part of a family here. Your Son, Jesus, grew up as a part of a family at Nazareth. By his presence**

he blessed the home of Mary, Martha, and Lazarus at Bethany. Now we pray that you will make this room a place of blessing; here may it become a haven of rest, and a place of joy. "O Lord, support us all the day long, until the shadows lengthen and the evening comes, and the busy world is hushed, and the fever of life is over, and our work is done. Then in your mercy grant us a safe lodging, and a rest, and peace at last." Amen.

A Service for Upholding a Resident Moving from Independent Living to Nursing Care

LEADER: We come together to ask God's blessing on _____ as he/she makes this move to Room _____.

We know all of life has its transitions and turning points. What God said through Joshua to the Israelites is the word he/she needs to hear today.

"Have I not commanded you? Be strong and of good courage; do not be afraid, nor be dismayed, for the Lord your God is with you wherever you go" (Joshua 1:9, NKJV).

A Litany of Intercession

LEADER: Gracious God, whose loving hand has been on us throughout life and whose presence is ever with us; we pray at this moment for _____. Give him/her confidence in your care and ceaseless love as he/she moves into another phase of life.

OTHERS: Nothing can separate us from the love of God.

LEADER: In the name of Jesus Christ we pray for those who serve residents in this place; grant them compassion and staying power.

OTHERS: Hear our prayer, O God.

LEADER: Give courage, O God, to _____ your servant in his/her new room. Help him/her to know the support of friends and your care. Let him/her know that you will never forsake him/her.

OTHERS: Hear our prayer, O God and give us your peace. Amen.

A Memorial Service for Residents

Note: This service might be celebrated once a year, twice a year, or monthly. Staff members, residents, and family members of the deceased may be invited to attend the service.

Materials: A Bible, a candle for each person who has died, Memory Book, carnations or daisies— one flower for each person being remembered.

WELCOME: As we celebrate this service together we trust you will cherish the memory of those who have died, find space to grieve, and receive hope and comfort.

LEADER: Today is a time of memories for us as we pause to remember friends who have died in the past month (_____ months). They have passed from life with us to a better life beyond this world. They made their last home with us for a while, but now they are with God in the Father's house with many rooms.

STAFF MEMBER: *(Each person is named and a candle is lighted or a flower placed on an altar. Soft music may be played at this time.)* We light this candle, a symbol of the light of lives we remember. As it burns we remember the many pieces of light that they brought to our lives.

Litany of Remembrance
(Led by Staff Member or Resident)

LEADER: Almighty God, we remember our friends. We remember the goodness of their lives and the wisdom they imparted to us.

PEOPLE: Grant unto them eternal rest, O Lord, and let perpetual light shine upon them.

LEADER: We thank you for the privilege of caring for them in their final days . . . as long as we live, they live too. For now they are a part of us as we remember them.

PEOPLE: May their souls rest in peace.

LEADER: For family who grieve their loss, may they be consoled in their grief by the Lord who wept at the grave of his friend Lazarus.

PEOPLE: Lord, hear their prayer.

LEADER: Into your hand, O Lord, we humbly entrust our friends _____. In this life you embraced them with your love and care; now grant them eternal rest. Their days on this earth have ended; but their best days have just begun.

> Life is ever lord of death,
>   and love can never lose its own.
> Death is not extinguishing the light;
> It is putting out the lamp because the
>   dawn has come.

CLOSING SONG: "Blest Be the Tie That Binds"

BLESSING: "The LORD bless you and keep you; the LORD make his face to shine upon you and be gracious to you; the LORD lift up his countenance upon you, and give you peace" (Num. 6:24-26). Now and forever. Amen.